THE ABINGDON WORSHIP ANNUAL

2005

CONTEMPORARY & TRADITIONAL
RESOURCES FOR WORSHIP LEADERS

The

ABINGDON

WORSHIP

Annual

2005

EDITED BY MARY J. SCIFRES & B. J. BEU
FOREWORD BY LEONARD SWEET

Abingdon Press
Nashville

THE ABINGDON WORSHIP ANNUAL 2005
CONTEMPORARY AND TRADITIONAL RESOURCES FOR WORSHIP LEADERS

Copyright © 2004 by Abingdon Press

This book is printed on recycled, acid-free, elemental-chlorine–free paper.

ISBN 0-687-00069-6
ISSN 1545-9322

04 05 06 07 08 09 10 11 12 13—10 9 8 7 6 5 4 3 2 1

MANUFACTURED IN THE UNITED STATES OF AMERICA

CONTENTS

109165

OCTOBER

NOVEMBER

DECEMBER

FOREWORD

ZIP It
by Leonard Sweet

A ll worship leaders engage in some final spiritual calisthenics before going out to meet their Maker every week. Some are intensely private, others are shared with our fellow worship leaders.

I shall never forget the ritual of the chaplain of one small Christian college. Before we walked out together into the sanctuary, we paused by the door as he said, "May I have a word of prayer with you?" Before I had finished replying, "I'd appreciate that very much," he had dropped on his knees, pulled out a handkerchief from his back pocket, and began shining my shoes as he prayed, "O Lord, as I wash my brother's feet, anoint his head with the oil of your Spirit, that he may offer your word from tip to toe for your people this day." It has been the most moving pre-worship calisthenics so far in my ministry.

I call my own spiritual calisthenic "ZIP." ZIP is an acronym for three body-mind-spirit push-ups. "Z" is for *zipper*. I have heard too many stories of worship leaders who failed to check their zippers (or blouses) not to start with this little exercise.

Then comes the letter "I," which stands for *image*. There are three parts to image: tongue, teeth, and eyes. *Tongue* twister exercises (my standards are "three short sword sheaths," "lovely lemon liniment," and "seashells by the seashore") get your mouth moist and your tongue under control. *Teeth* reminds me to check for food particles (in my case poppy seeds since I'm always eating poppy seed bagels). One of the more embarrassing moments in my ministry was preaching on television with black diamonds sparkling in my teeth whenever I smiled. *Eyes* reminds me to eye myself in the mirror to make sure all the other body parts are put together and arranged properly.

The "P" in ZIP is the most important. It stands for *Prayer* and puts the acronym ZIP to work. Reciting Psalm 51:10, I pray to be zippered in a "right spirit" as I speak. I also pray to zipper my own thoughts and desires and to zip myself in the promise of this verse from Deuteronomy 18:18 (NIV): "I will put my words in [your] mouth, and [you] will tell them everything I command [you]."

Worship leaders speak with a divine voice, under penalty of death (Deuteronomy 18:15-20). Worship leaders are intermediaries between heaven and earth, bridging this world and the next, the invisible and the visible. For worship to be true, the Holy Spirit must live in the bloodstream with the red blood cells of God's Word running in every vein.

But worship planners and leaders speak with not only a divine voice but also a communal voice. Your voice is not your own. It is magnified and megaphoned by the communion of saints. We are not the only ones present when we speak in worship. We bring unseen others with us. We bring grandmothers and grandfathers, aunts and uncles. We bring Matthew, Mark, Luke, and John. We bring Peter and Paul, Mary and Martha, John Wesley and Mother Teresa. Are we zipping up ourselves to make room for them?

This volume is intended to help you fill your worship space with the rush of holiness. Some of the best practitioners of the art and craft of worship planning have been asked to contribute their creativity. Bring them with you and feel the rush of history fill the room.

INTRODUCTION

Worship Planning: Artwork Always in Process

Worship planning is hardly a feat of engineering. More like pieces of beautiful artwork, worship planning differs from worship service to worship service, from planner to planner, from week to week. Worship planning involves passion and creativity, imagination and openness. Worship planning begins with prayer and study and is undergirded by scripture and theology. The plan may begin months in advance, but seldom is the final plan written into a script until a few days before the event. And even then, the plan is simply a script. Until the play is in motion, when the worship service is occurring, the worship plan is nothing more than a guideline for rehearsal. But the performance of the worship service becomes the piece of art. It comes to fruition not as a set design, but rather a flowing, interactive piece of theater, involving God and God's worshipers, prompted into the play by worship leaders, preachers, musicians, and planners. And so, worship is truly a piece of artwork, like live theater or music, always in process, changing with the participants and the listener. And in all of this process, the Holy One is living and moving in our worship—from the first seed of planning to the final breath of the benediction or the last note of the postlude.

As you begin the seminal work of crafting your services of worship together, you will find *The Abingdon Worship Annual* an invaluable resource. Prayers, words, and ideas

11

are here to be integrated into your process of worship planning. We know that the words written here may take a different shape under your penmanship. The thoughts expressed here may take a different form in your message and method of planning. The dreams we have for this book include that process, complete with your thoughts, your dreams, and your plans. But most of all, the dreams we have for this book include the work of the Holy One, who calls us into worship and yearns for us to be one with God in our worship experiences.

Within this text, you will find suggestions for Sundays and holy days to help plan your corporate worship services. Each entry includes: Calls to Worship, Praise Sentences or Contemporary Gathering Words, Opening Prayers, Prayers of Confession or Unison Prayers, and Benedictions or Closing Prayers.

The Abingdon Worship Annual was written to complement *The Abingdon Preaching Annual*. In addition, *The Abingdon Worship Annual* can be used with *Prepare! A Weekly Worship Planbook for Pastors and Musicians* or *The United Methodist Music and Worship Planner*. As pastors, we recognize that few worship planners have as much time and creative energy to spend planning their services of worship as we would like. Just as *Prepare!* and *The United Methodist Music and Worship Planner* are tremendous time savers in planning music, *The Abingdon Worship Annual* provides pastors and worship planners the liturgical elements to put a complete service of worship together. Just as *The Abingdon Preaching Annual* is intended to spark your creative energies for preaching, so is this resource intended to spark your creative energies for worship planning.

In this resource, we have included more than just traditional words for worship. For the worship planner or preacher involved in nontraditional worship styles, many ideas in this text are specifically for your use.

Calls to Worship refer to those traditional words that gather God's people together as they prepare to worship God. Often called "Greetings" or "Gathering Words," these words are typically read responsively. Some of the Contemporary Gathering Words listed in each resource may also be helpful as Calls to Worship in a traditional or blended setting. As with all responsive readings, think creatively as you plan your services. While it is simplest to have a single leader read the words in light print, with the congregation responding by reading the words in bold print, it can be effective to have several people, or even groups of people, lead these calls. Using the choir, a youth group, or a small prayer group participate in responsive readings adds variety and vitality to your services. Some congregations enjoy responding to one another: women to men, right side to left side, children to parents. Experiment with a variety of options and see how these words might be most meaningful in calling your congregation together to worship the Holy One.

On the nontraditional side of opening worship, we offer Contemporary Gathering Words and Praise Sentences. Leaders who find extemporaneous speaking difficult will find these entries particularly helpful when leading worship.

Like more formal Calls to Worship, Gathering Words are often read responsively. Unlike more formal Calls to Worship, however, Gathering Words tend to use simpler language and be more repetitive in nature. You may copy these Gathering Words onto an overhead transparency to help your congregation read responsively without being tied to a bulletin. If your congregation does not care to read words aloud, consider using two leaders to speak in "call and response" format. Or, allow the song team or band members to act as responders to the worship leader, echoing the call and response tradition of African American Christians.

While many of the Praise Sentences provided in this resource are easily spoken by one leader, using the call and response format is an option. In praise settings, worshipers are often willing to respond in echo form, repeating the words or phrases spoken by the worship leader. Echoing the same words and phrases several times can be highly effective. The Praise Sentences in this resource are not intended to limit you, but rather to free you to lead in a more informal style, where appropriate.

Opening Prayers in this resource are varied in form, but typically invoke God's presence in worship. Some are more informal than others, and some are more general than formal invocations. Many can be adapted for later use in the worship service, if that suits your needs. For simplicity's sake, we have grouped them all into the category of Opening Prayers. Again, in traditional worship, it is common to print these prayers and recite them in unison. However, in nontraditional settings, you may wish to print them for solo voice or simply share them with worship leaders for their adaptation as they offer opening prayers informally.

Prayers of Confession and Words of Assurance follow many different formats. At times, the Words of Assurance are actually contained in the prayer. When they are not, you may wish to use Words of Assurance from a previous day's suggested resources or from a favorite scripture of assurance. Some scriptures, particularly in the Easter season, did not lend themselves to confession and, thus, such prayers are absent.

Prayers take many forms in this resource. Some are in the form of a Collect. Prayers need not be spoken in unison, but may be spoken alone by a single leader or led by a small group. Some prayers may even be adapted as Opening or Closing Prayers. They may be revised into call and response format. In all cases, we have sought to provide words that can easily be spoken by a large congregation in unison. For the sake of consistency, such entries have been given the title Unison Prayer. Again, this title is not meant to limit your use, but simply to categorize prayers that you may use in any format that works for your worship setting.

Benedictions, sometimes known as Blessings or Words of Dismissal, are included in each entry. Some work best in call and response format; others seem more appropriate as a solitary blessing from the worship leader. Choose a format best suited to your congregation: whether in unison, by a worship leader alone, or in a call and response format.

Many litanies, prayers, and calls to worship in *The Abingdon Worship Annual 2005* intersperse direct quotations from scripture with lines of text for other sources. In order to facilitate the ease of use with this resource, we have chosen not to indicate in the prayers and other worship resources where scripture is being directly quoted and where it is not.

This is our second year of publishing *The Abingdon Worship Annual*. Please let us hear from you as you work with this resource. In future volumes, we hope to integrate your ideas on improving this resource while maintaining those features that are most helpful to you. We are eager to learn what does and does not work for you.

As you design your worship service, we invite you to read through the scriptures for each day. Then read through the liturgical suggestions in this resource that speak to those readings. Use this resource as the Spirit guides you, letting God's Word flow through you and the members of your worship planning team. Allow the artwork of worship planning to become its own process, as the Holy Spirit, truly our worship muse, works in this process with you. Trust God's guidance and enjoy a wonderful year of worship and praise with your congregations!

Enjoy this resource, and enjoy the year ahead. We wish you God's blessings as you participate in the art of worship. As you share Christ's word and offer experiences of the Spirit in your worship, may the Holy Spirit shower creativity and beauty into your process of planning and enacting that worship. Blessings on the journey!

MARY J. SCIFRES AND B. J. BEU

JANUARY 1, 2005

Watch Night/New Year

B. J. Beu

COLOR
White

SCRIPTURE READINGS
Ecclesiastes 3:1-13; Psalm 8; Revelation 21:1-6*a*; Matthew 25:31-46

THEME IDEAS
What time is it? This is the question we ask ourselves at the beginning of each new year. Is it a time to plant or a time to harvest? A time to throw away stones or a time to gather stones together? Is it a time to behold the new Jerusalem and see God among us or a time to see the weeping and pain of those who have no hope? Today's scriptures invite exploration of these themes as they offer glimpses of the hand of God in every time of our lives.

CALL TO WORSHIP (ECCLESIASTES 3)
God comes to us in seasons of plenty
and in seasons of want.
    We give thanks for the gifts of God!
God is with us in times of birth
and at the moment of death.
    We give thanks for the gifts of God!
God nurtures us in periods of growth

and in times of decay.
We give thanks for the gifts of God!
Gd gives us memories of the past
and hope for the future.
We give thanks for the gifts of God!
God gives us everything we need.
We give thanks for the gifts of God!

CALL TO WORSHIP (PSALM 8)

O God, how majestic is your name in all the earth!
Your glory is higher than the heavens!
When we ponder the works of your hands,
the moon and all the countless stars,
who are we that you are mindful of us?
Who are we that you care for us?
Yet you have given us stewardship of your creation.
You entreat us to care for your creatures.
O God, how majestic is your name in all the earth!

CONTEMPORARY GATHERING WORDS (MATTHEW 25)

Christ warns us, "I was hungry and you gave me no
food, I was thirsty and you gave me nothing to drink."
Lord, when did we see you hungry or thirsty?
"I was a stranger and you did not welcome me, naked
and you did not give me clothing, sick and in prison and
you did not visit me."
**Lord, when did we see you a stranger or naked or
sick or in prison?**
"Every day, you saw me in the streets, in the news, and in
your church newsletters, yet you saw me not, for you saw
only the faces of my children, your sisters and brothers."
Is it too late for us?
"It is never too late. See with new eyes and love with new
hearts and you will be saved."
Thanks be to God!

PRAISE SENTENCES (ECCLESIASTES 3)

A new day has dawned.
Praise the Lord!
A new year has begun.
Praise the Lord!
Praise the God of new beginnings.
Praise the Lord!

OPENING PRAYER (REVELATION 21)

Eternal God,
in whom all things are made new,
be our Alpha and Omega,
our beginning and our end.
You dwell with us
and wipe away our tears.
You invite us to leave behind our pain and despair
and live anew in the glory of your presence.
Keep our eyes upon your heavenly city,
that our vision might be true
and our actions full of hopeful expectation.
Be our God,
that we may be your people. Amen.

OPENING PRAYER (NEW YEAR)

God of inexhaustible possibilities,
come to us this day,
as we ponder what lies before us
in the year ahead.
Teach us to see opportunities for growth
in the struggles that lie before us.
Help us find moments of grace and forgiveness
in the face of ridicule and scorn.
Be a light to our path,
that we may walk confidently in your ways,
through Jesus Christ our hope and redeemer.
Amen.

PRAYER OF CONFESSION (MATTHEW 25)

Merciful God,
> we worship you with our lips
> but fail to see you in the lives
> > of our fellow creatures.

We feel secure in our bounty,
> while neglecting those in want.

We are proud of our accomplishments,
> and too easily blame those in need
> > for their lack of success in life.

Transform our hearts to see you anew:
> in those who are hungry and thirsty,
> in those who are strangers to us,
> in those who lack clothing,
> and in those who are sick or imprisoned.

We ask this in the name of your Son,
> who teaches us to treat each other
> > as beloved sisters and brothers. Amen.

BENEDICTION (ECCLESIASTES 3, REVELATION 21)

Go with the blessings of the One
who gives us the seasons of our lives.
> **We go with God's blessings!**

Go with the blessings of the One
who wipes away every tear.
> **We go with God's blessings!**

Go with the blessings of the One
who is our eternal home.
> **We go with God's blessings!**

JANUARY 2, 2005

Second Sunday After Christmas

B. J. Beu

COLOR
White

SCRIPTURE READINGS
Jeremiah 31:7-14; Psalm 147:12-20; Ephesians 1:3-14; John 1:(1-9) 10-18

THEME IDEAS
This is a time to rejoice in the vastness of God's salvation. Jeremiah invites us to sing and shout with gladness, for God is gathering the lost remnants of Israel that have been scattered abroad and is bringing them home. The psalmist praises God for the gift of peace. And the epistle blesses God that the followers of Christ have been adopted as God's own children and given the Holy Spirit to guide them. Finally, John makes clear the source of these manifold blessings: the very Logos of God, which was in the beginning with God, creating all that was and is and is to be. Those who follow Christ, follow the Light of all light and the source of all hope.

CALL TO WORSHIP (PSALM 147)
Praise the LORD, O Jerusalem!
Praise your God, O Zion!
  Praise the Lord!
Praise the Lord, O people of God!

Sing praises to the Holy One of Israel!
Sing praises to our God Most High!
Shout for joy, you who call on the name of the Lord!
Rejoice in the peace of God's reign!
We rejoice in God's tender mercy!
Sing praises to God!
Praise the Lord!

CALL TO WORSHIP (JEREMIAH 31)

Where are God's faithful who were scattered abroad?
God is calling them home, to be with God's people.
Where are the blind and the lame,
and those who lost their way?
God is binding their wounds and guiding their feet.
Where are the comfortless and those who grieve?
God is turning their sorrow into joy.
Are we prepared to worship the One who calls us home,
binds our wounds, and comforts our sorrow?
**We have come to be God's people,
and to worship the Lord.**

CALL TO WORSHIP (EPHESIANS 1)

Christ has blessed us with every spiritual gift.
Blessed be the Lord!
Christ has adopted us as God's own children.
Blessed be the Lord!
Christ has sealed us into God's salvation
through the power of the Holy Spirit.
Blessed be the Lord!
Christ has offered us an eternal inheritance
in God's redemptive love.
Blessed be the Lord!

CONTEMPORARY GATHERING WORDS (JOHN 1)

Christ is our Light.
Rejoice and be glad!

Christ is the light of all peoples.
Rejoice and be glad!
Christ is a beacon in the darkness.
Rejoice and be glad!
The Light has come.
Rejoice and be glad!

PRAISE SENTENCES (JOHN 1)

The creator of all things is with us.
The spirit of truth is in our midst!
The true light is with us!
The way of salvation is in our midst!

OPENING PRAYER (JEREMIAH 31)

God of promise and hope,
    you stretch out your hand and the mighty fall.
You call to us,
    drawing us back from the pit
        and rescuing us from exile.
You never abandon us.
Help us to look beyond our own interests,
    to the needs of the blind and lame,
    the weeping and the anguished.
Set our voices free,
    to celebrate with singing and shouts of praise
        our deliverance from the forces of death
        and destruction.
Teach us the language of sheer joy,
    that the world may know
        that you are the Lord God Almighty. Amen.

OPENING PRAYER (EPHESIANS 1)

Eternal God,
    you bless us with your precepts
        and watch over our faltering footsteps.
Through the richness of your grace,

and the love of your son Jesus Christ,
you have forgiven our transgressions
    and adopted us to be your own children.
You have given us the gospel of your salvation,
    and fitted us for heaven.
May your Holy Spirit perfect our lives,
    that we might be worthy of your blessings.
Through Jesus Christ our Lord. Amen.

PRAYER OF CONFESSION (JOHN 1)
Holy God,
    you sent your Son into the world,
    that we might no longer walk in darkness.
We confess that we have not always loved the light.
You sent your Son into the world
    that we might become children of God.
We confess that we have often forsaken our birthright.
Forgive our fascination with the darkness,
    and grant us the power to be born anew
        in your holy image.
We ask this in the name of the One
    who came into the world, not to condemn the world,
    but to save it. Amen.

WORDS OF ASSURANCE (EPHESIANS 1)
God, who raised Christ from the dead,
    has chosen us for adoption.
As God's adopted children,
    we have an inheritance of God's salvation
    and the promise of eternal life.

BENEDICTION (JOHN 1)
Go with the blessings of God.
    We go with God's blessings!
Go with the blessings of the one true Light.
    We go with God's blessings!
Go with the blessings of the Lord of life.
    We go with God's blessings!

JANUARY 6, 2005

Epiphany of the Lord
Brian Wren

COLOR
White

SCRIPTURE READINGS
Isaiah 60:1-6; Psalm 72:1-7, 10-14; Ephesians 3:1-12; Matthew 2:1-12

THEME IDEAS
It is hard to privatize Epiphany. Isaiah hails the divine light that dispels darkness over nations and peoples, and brings exiles home. The psalmist praises the One who legislates peace, social justice (righteousness), and deliverance from oppressive violence. Ephesians heralds a divine mystery now to be revealed to "rulers and authorities" whose heavenly location parallels events on earth. Matthew shows "wise" men naive enough to ask a despot for travel directions to his successor. As always, we see the light most clearly when we name and meet the darkness.

CALL TO WORSHIP (ISAIAH 60, PSALM 72, MATTHEW 2)
Let us worship God.
Darkness covers the earth

and thick darkness the peoples.
The poor cry out for bread
and the weak suffer violence.
But God's light shines
through an infant child.
We have seen his star at its rising
and have come to pay him homage.
He is like showers that water the earth,
like rain that falls on the mown grass.
Thanks be to God!

CALL TO WORSHIP (EPHESIANS 3)

Come and meet a mystery,
hidden from the dawn of time,
now revealed among us.
Come and hear good news:
Christ has boundless riches.
Everyone may share them.
Say to all the people,
to rulers and authorities:
No one is discarded.
Everyone is welcome. Alleluia!

CONTEMPORARY GATHERING WORDS (MATTHEW 2)

When a child is born, light shines.
When Jesus is born, hope dawns,
and love arrives.
Newborn Jesus, shine upon us.
From your cradle and your cross
give us love and life.

PRAISE SENTENCES (ISAIAH 60)

When the light of God shines
we shall see it and be radiant.

Our hearts shall thrill and rejoice!
**Glorious God, shine in our hearts
and fill us with praise.**

OPENING PRAYER (MATTHEW 2)
Infant Christ, whose light shines out
not from a palace
but from a village woman's lap,
shine on us today
through the youngest and the least,
that we may open our treasures
and give them precious gifts
in your name.

OPENING PRAYER OR PRAYER OF CONFESSION AND LAMENT (MATTHEW 2, PSALM 72)
Holy God, we confess and lament
the violence of our world
and our collective fascination
with military might,
righteous revenge,
merciless justice,
and national pride.
Shine on us
from the cradle of your vulnerability
that forgiveness, mercy, and kindness
may glow and grow among us
through Jesus Christ. Amen.

BENEDICTION
Go out as one body,
Christ's body.
Love.
Forgive.
Show mercy.

Make peace.
And tell the good news
of Christ, the world's light. Amen.

BENEDICTION

People of God, go out.
Cradle in your hearts
the great mystery
of reconciling love,
that it may take root and flourish
within you, among you, and beyond you,
through Jesus Christ. Amen.

Copyright © 2003 by Brian Wren

JANUARY 9, 2005

First Sunday After the Epiphany/ Baptism of the Lord

Mary J. Scifres

COLOR

White

SCRIPTURE READINGS

Isaiah 42:1-9; Psalm 29; Acts 10:34-43; Matthew 3:13-17

THEME IDEAS

The presence of water is shown as both power and grace in today's readings from Psalm 29 and Matthew 3. The strength of God's love can emerge as a primary focus as these two readings are integrated into a service of baptism or a congregational renewal of baptism. However, Isaiah and Acts intermingle the power of God's righteousness and call to justice with the grace that Christ offers to all who believe. As these different aspects of Christ's ministry and God's presence in our baptism arise, they may elicit a merging of themes or a focus on one scripture for this day.

CALL TO WORSHIP (ISAIAH 42, MATTHEW 3)

We have come, yearning for the Spirit of God.
    The Spirit of God is upon us.
We have come, yearning for the justice of Christ.

The Spirit of justice is ours to share.
We have come, yearning to be God's people.
We are the people of the covenant,
God's beloved children.
Come, Christ calls us here, to seek justice,
and to be the children of God.

CALL TO WORSHIP (PSALM 29)

Praise the Lord—the God of glory and strength!
We listen for the sound of God's glory and strength.
Hear the voice of power and majesty!
We look for the signs of God's power and majesty.
See the gifts of God's mercy and grace.
We worship the Lord—
the God of glory and strength,
power and majesty, mercy and grace.
Thanks be to God!

CONTEMPORARY GATHERING WORDS (ISAIAH 42)

The Holy One calls us into righteousness
Come, now is the time to worship!
Jesus takes us by the hand.
Come, now is the time to worship!
Christ brings light into the darkness.
Come, now is the time to worship!
Our God comes to us, bringing new hope.
Come, now is the time to worship!

PRAISE SENTENCES (PSALM 29)

The voice of the Lord is mighty!
Praise God's glory and strength!
The voice of the Lord is mighty!
Praise God's glory and strength!

PRAISE SENTENCES (PSALM 29)

Our God is a mighty God! Our God is a mighty God!

OPENING PRAYER (PSALM 29, MATTHEW 3)

Beloved One, send your Spirit upon us this day.
Open the heavens and pour out your mercy and love,
    that we might know your mercy and love.
Enter into our worship,
    that we might hear your voice and respond to your call
        with the same love and mercy you have shown us.
In the name of your beloved child, Christ Jesus, we pray.
Amen.

OPENING PRAYER (ISAIAH 42)

God of power and might,
    be with us in this time of worship.
As we seek your justice,
    guide our hands and our hearts.
As we live out your calling,
    walk with us and strengthen our spirits.
May our eyes be open,
    our chains be unbound,
    and our lives be filled with newfound promise.
Amen.

PRAYER OF CONFESSION (PSALM 29, ACTS 10, MATTHEW 3)

Merciful God,
    forgive us when we doubt the strength and breadth
        of your love.
Forgive us when we draw lines and divisions
    where you show no partiality.
Forgive us when we doubt your promise of new life
    and pursue our own lives of destruction
        and disappointment.
Forgive us most of all, beloved parent of us all,
    when we forget that all of your people on earth
        are your beloved children,
        blessed by your Holy Spirit.
Forgive us, we pray. Amen.

WORDS OF ASSURANCE (ACTS 10)

Everyone, *everyone,* who believes in Christ
receives forgiveness of sins through Christ's holy name.

BENEDICTION (ISAIAH 42)

The former things have come to pass,
but now God promises a new thing:
justice and mercy, righteousness and love,
hope and healing.
Lead lives fitting of this promise, and be transformed.
Amen.

BENEDICTION (ISAIAH 42, MATTHEW 3)

Go forth, beloved children of God,
claiming the blessings of life in Christ:
new life, new hope, new beginnings;
justice and righteousness for a world in need.
We go as God's beloved,
living new lives with new hope for a new world.

JANUARY 16, 2005

Second Sunday After the Epiphany
Mary J. Scifres

COLOR
Green

SCRIPTURE READINGS
Isaiah 49:1-7; Psalm 40:1-11; 1 Corinthians 1:1-9; John 1:29-42

THEME IDEAS
Today begins the first ordinary season (also known as Kingdomtide) of the church year, the period in which the lections run continuously through books of the Bible. (This contrasts with the holy seasons with their inter-locking unity of theme and purpose.) Even so, this season after the Epiphany begins with a common focus on God's Spirit and God's call, constantly prodding us forward into unity with God and ministry with God's world.

CALL TO WORSHIP OR CONTEMPORARY GATHERING WORDS (PSALM 40)
Wait patiently for the Lord.
   Wait? I spend the whole week waiting!
Wait patiently for the Lord.
   Patiently? I'm ready for God right now!

Wait patiently for the Lord.
Is it true what they say:
"Happy are those who trust in God"?
Wait patiently for the Lord.
Wait patiently for the Lord? Hmm . . .
Wait patiently for the Lord. God's steadfast love
and faithfulness are with us even now.
Now that's worth waiting for!

CALL TO WORSHIP (1 CORINTHIANS 1)

Come, saints of the church.
Come, Father God, who calls us here.
Come, sinners of the world.
Come, Redeemer Christ, who gives us grace.
Come, lovers of all of life.
Come, Sister Spirit, who lives and breathes with us.
Come in the name of the Lord!

CONTEMPORARY GATHERING WORDS (ISAIAH 49)

Listen to me, you coastlands and oceans,
you people from far away! The Lord has called us here!
God will make us a light to the nations!
We are servants and friends, reflections of God,
showing Christ's love to the world.
God will make us a light to the nations!
Gathered as one, honored and called,
we are strengthened by God, the redeeming One.
God will make us a light to the nations!

CONTEMPORARY GATHERING WORDS (1 CORINTHIANS 1)

Give thanks to God always for the grace of God
you have received in Christ Jesus.
God has strengthened and blessed us all
in Christ Jesus.

Our gifts are blessings, budding and growing,
as we build the body of Christ.
> **Christ will strengthen and bless us all,**
> **both now and forevermore.**
Our God is faithful, calling us into this place of worship.

CONTEMPORARY GATHERING WORDS (JOHN 1)

What are you looking for?
A teacher, a preacher?
A healer, a savior?
A miracle, a dream?
Faith or hope?
Joy or love?
Come and see.
For in Christ Jesus, you will find all of these things here.

CONTEMPORARY GATHERING WORDS (JOHN 1)

What are you looking for?
Where are you staying?
Where are you going?
Whom do you seek?
Why do you question?
Come and see how the answers can change.

PRAISE SENTENCES (PSALM 40)

God's works are too great to number!
The stars are alive, bursting flames of brilliant light.
Beyond count, yet fewer than the great works of God.
We will sing God's praise as we remember our joy,
for nothing compares to the promise we have in God.

PRAISE SENTENCES (1 CORINTHIANS 1)

Grace and peace, my friends!
I give thanks to God, for God has called us here!
Grace and peace, my friends!
Let's give thanks to God, for God has called us here!

CALL TO PRAYER (PSALM 40)

Wait patiently for the Lord, who hears our cries.
Sing the songs of love and praises to God,
who listens to all our needs.
Put your trust in God, who does wondrous deeds
and hearkens to our tiniest needs.
With God's Word in our lives
and Christ's love in our hearts,
we turn to God in prayer.

OPENING PRAYER (1 CORINTHIANS 1)

Faithful, loving God,
strengthen us in this hour.
Nurture our lives
and bless us we pray.
You have given us every spiritual gift to be your church.
Help us trust that your gifts will suffice.
As we worship,
let your Spirit move through us.
Gather us into one body as your church,
and send us forth in the ministry of your love.
In faithful trust, we pray. Amen.

OPENING PRAYER (PSALM 40, JOHN 1)

Lamb of God,
shepherd us into your pastures.
Save us from paths
that deter us from faith and hope.
Preserve us from attitudes
that inhibit joy and love.
Lead us into trust in your Word
and hope in your world.
Guide us into the joy of your love. Amen.

BENEDICTION (1 CORINTHIANS 1)

We have been strengthened by Christ
and blessed by God.

We lack no gift or talent
as we wait for God's reign to arrive.
But wait! The reign of God is coming and now is!
We are the reign of God
when we use our gifts for love.
God will strengthen us to the end,
and call us along the way.
We go into the world, answering the call,
so that others may find the strength
and the blessing we have found.

BENEDICTION (ISAIAH 49)

Listen, friends and strangers, near and far,
God has called us here!
Listen to the Spirit's call,
for God now sends us forth!
Go as a light to the nations,
taking salvation both near and far.
We go as the redeemed of God,
that salvation may be brought to all.

JANUARY 23, 2005

Third Sunday After the Epiphany
Sara Dunning Lambert

COLOR

Green

SCRIPTURE READINGS

Isaiah 9:1-4; Psalm 27:1, 4-9; 1 Corinthians 1:10-18; Matthew 4:12-23

THEME IDEAS

The imagery of light shining in the darkness brings hope during these gray days of January. Isaiah chose darkness to represent the burden of oppression, an image that connects easily to our personal lives. Shining light on our burdens, God lifts their weight from our shoulders. In the Psalm, we read that hope in the Lord is our light and our salvation and removes all fear. Paul, in his letter to the Corinthians, speaks of the unity needed to preach the gospel. Following Isaiah, Matthew equates Jesus with God's light shining in the darkness. In our search for the light of God, we seek God's favor, knowing that in God we find shelter, refuge, and hope.

CALL TO WORSHIP (ISAIAH 9, PSALM 27, MATTHEW 4)

With heavy burdens we come to you.
We have seen a great light!
Out of darkness we come seeking you, O Lord.

We have seen a great light!
You are our light and our salvation.
We have seen a great light!
We have no fear in the strength of your shelter.
We have seen a great light!
God's kingdom is near!
We have seen a great light! Amen!

CALL TO WORSHIP (PSALM 27, MATTHEW 4, ISAIAH 9)

We come to worship you Lord,
seeking refuge from doubt and freedom from fear.
We yearn to live in the shelter of your presence.
Lord, you break the bonds of our oppression
with the piercing clarity of your light.
You lift our burdens, surrounding us with hope.
Let those who have experienced darkness
feel the promise of your eternal radiance.
**We shout for joy, secure in the knowledge
of your love. Amen!**

CONTEMPORARY GATHERING WORDS (1 CORINTHIANS 1, MATTHEW 4)

We gather together as brothers and sisters in Christ.
We will follow Jesus.
Christ will teach us to fish for people.
We will follow Jesus.
We are united in purpose to spread the good news!
We will follow Jesus.

PRAISE SENTENCES (ISAIAH 9)

God shines a great light in the darkness for all to see.
Rejoice, for the Lord has broken the bonds of oppression!

PRAISE SENTENCES (PSALM 27)

Rejoice, for the Lord is our shelter,
a refuge against all enemies.

Praise God who hides us, protects us,
   and nurtures us in times of trouble.
Our gracious Lord hears our cry.
Do not be afraid!

OPENING PRAYER (PSALM 27)

Through our darkness,
   we seek the path to your dwelling place, O Lord.
You, who are our light and salvation,
   provide us shelter from harm,
   and cover us with hope.
We come seeking your face,
   knowing that you hear when we call
      and hearken to our aid with grace and love.
Amen.

OPENING PRAYER (MATTHEW 4)

Loving Christ, you beckoned your disciples:
   "Follow me, and I will make you fish for people."
We yearn to follow the example of Peter and Andrew,
   James and John, leaving our nets to follow you.
Instill in us the simplicity and passion of faith
   to proclaim the good news to all in your name. Amen.

BENEDICTION (ISAIAH 9, PSALM 27, MATTHEW 4)

We go out into the light, fearing the darkness no more.
   The light of Christ is shining!
Our burdens are lifted, we rejoice with thanksgiving.
   The light of Christ is shining!
May God's shelter surround us with peace and love.
   The light of Christ is shining!

BENEDICTION (1 CORINTHIANS 1, MATTHEW 4)

United in love, we proclaim Christ's gospel for all to hear.
Bound together in Christ,
   we strive together to become fishers of people,
   that everyone may experience the joy of Christ's love.
The kingdom of God has come! Amen!

JANUARY 30, 2005

Fourth Sunday After the Epiphany
Mary J. Scifres

COLOR
Green

SCRIPTURE READINGS
Micah 6:1-8; Psalm 15; 1 Corinthians 1:18-31; Matthew 5:1-12

THEME IDEAS
Humility and mercy arise throughout this lesson. The wisdom of the world, the safety of personal success, and salvation through works are all negated in comparison to the love and mercy of God. As lovers of God, we are called to embrace and live this same love and mercy, shown in humility and patience. In our love and mercy, we will find the true blessings of God.

CALL TO WORSHIP (MICAH 6)
With what shall we come before our God?
We come with burdens and worries.
With what shall we come before our God?
We come with scattered minds and thoughts.
With what shall we come before our God?
We come with schedules and deadlines.
With what shall we come before our God?
We come with children and friends,
loved ones and neighbors.

With what shall we come before our God?
We come with offerings and ministries,
Sunday school lessons and volunteer commitments.
With what shall we come before our God?
We come with thankful hearts and yearning souls.
With what shall we come before our God?
We come with a desire to do justly,
for we love mercy.
Come, my friends, let us walk humbly with our God.

CONTEMPORARY GATHERING WORDS (MATTHEW 5)

Come, all who are feeling beaten down by the world.
We will be blessed by God.
Come, all who are full of sorrow and grief.
We will be blessed by God.
Come, all who are humble and meek.
We will be blessed by God.
Come, all who are hungry and thirst for righteousness.
We will be blessed by God.
Come, all who are merciful and kind.
We will be blessed by God.
Come, all who are pure in heart.
We will be blessed by God.
Come, all who create peace and hope in a world of strife.
We will be blessed by God.
Come, all who are weary and burdened.
We will be blessed by God.
Come, all who are struggling and working.
We will be blessed by God.
Come, all who yearn to know Christ.
For here, we will all be blessed by God!

PRAISE SENTENCES (MICAH 6)

Our God is an awesome God of justice and mercy.
Praise be to God!
Our God is an awesome God of justice and mercy.
Praise be to God!

42

PRAISE SENTENCES (1 CORINTHIANS 1, MATTHEW 5)

Our life is in you, Lord!
Our life is in you, Lord!
Our grace is in you, Lord!
Our grace is in you, Lord!
Our hope is in you, Lord!
Our hope is in you, Lord!
Our trust is in you, Lord!
Our trust is in you, Lord!
Thanks be to God, who gives the victory!

OPENING PRAYER (MICAH 6)

O loving One of mercy and justice,
    we come into your presence this day
        with hearts full of the past week.
Help us to lay aside our anxious minds
    as you lift our worries and burdens.
Guide us into your presence,
    that we might know your mercy and justice,
    not only in this place
        but in all of the corners of our lives.
Walk alongside us, Christ Jesus,
    that we might know humility and mercy
        in our journey of faith.
Help us to know you more.
In the name of Christ, we pray. Amen.

PRAYER OF CONFESSION (MICAH 6, PSALM 15)

Gracious and merciful God,
    we never seem to measure up to Christian perfection.
Try as we may,
    we do not walk blamelessly on this earth.
Forgive us when we do things we know to be wrong,
    and when we speak things we know to be untrue.
Help us, loving God,

to honor you and to walk with you
　by doing no evil on this earth.
Teach us to walk in humility and mercy with your people,
　and share your justice and grace with your world.
Amen.

PRAYER OF CONFESSION (1 CORINTHIANS 1)

O Wisdom from on high,
　help us to discern your wisdom.
When we pursue the foolish truths of this world,
　forgive us.
When we stumble over the message of the cross,
　help us to walk upright.
When we ignore your wise guidance,
　lead us back onto your path.
And when we neglect your guidance,
　open our ears,
　　that we might heed your voice
　　　and answer your call.
Forgive us and guide us, loving God.
Help us to find our source of life in you,
　through Christ Jesus. Amen.

BENEDICTION (1 CORINTHIANS 1)

Consider your own call, brothers and sisters.
God has chosen you, foolish and wise,
　to be disciples of the living Christ.
Go into the world, strengthened by Christ
　who is your wisdom and righteousness.

BENEDICTION (MATTHEW 5)

Blessed are you when you open your hearts to Jesus.
Go forth as the poor in spirit, the meek and humble,
　the merciful and pure.
Go forth, hungering and thirsting for righteousness,
　and you will be blessed by God!

FEBRUARY 6, 2005

Transfiguration Sunday
Nancy Crawford Holm

COLOR
White or Gold

SCRIPTURE READINGS
Exodus 24:12-18; Psalm 99; 2 Peter 1:16-21; Matthew 17:1-9

THEME IDEAS
Transfiguration Sunday is the last Sunday before Lent. It is a time to celebrate the revelation of Christ to people of faith, a time to connect the glory of God revealed to Moses on Sinai to the glory of God in Christ revealed to Jesus' disciples. It is also a time of transition from Jesus' work of teaching and healing to the journey of Lent. Themes could center around transformation, patriarchs and prophets (possibly including modern prophets), the mountaintop, one more mountain to climb, glory, and images of Christ.

CALL TO WORSHIP (PSALM 99)
The LORD is Sovereign.
Let the people tremble in awe.
God is enthroned between the cherubim.
Let the earth shake.
The LORD is great in Zion.

God is high above all peoples.
Come let us worship our glorious Lord.

CONTEMPORARY GATHERING WORDS

Let the radiance of Christ be evident among us:
in our songs and our words;
in our deepest thoughts and desires;
in the youthful and the experienced,
the exhausted and the energetic;
in the hungry and the scared.
We are here together.
We join our voices and our hearts in praise.

CONTEMPORARY GATHERING WORDS

We gather as witnesses to the transforming power of God.
Gather us in, God of yesterday, today, and tomorrow.
Alleluia, alleluia, alleluia!

PRAISE SENTENCES (PSALM 99)

Holy is our God! Mighty is the King of kings,
the lover of justice.
God has established justice and righteousness.
Extol the LORD our God. Worship at God's footstool.
Holy is our God!

OPENING PRAYER (MATTHEW 17)

Holy God, who revealed the Messiah on the mountain,
fill us with praise, overflowing with cheers
and mysterious visions.
Light our way; direct our course; and energize us,
for we have one more mountain to climb,
through Jesus Christ, who is the light. Amen.

OPENING PRAYER (EXODUS 24, MATTHEW 17)

God of the mountaintop and of the plain,
we remember today the Transfiguration of Jesus.

Glorious, mysterious, and shimmering with light,
   you know our hearts, our triumphs,
   and our disasters.
Take us as we are; love us as we are;
   join with us and transform us into your holy ones.
Amen.

BENEDICTION

Hear the words of hope set to music by Mozart:
   "The sun's golden splendour now sunders the night,
   And shatters the power of the evil one's might."
Let us live, die, and rise in the image and power of Christ.
Amen and Amen.
(Wolfgang Amadeus Mozart, *The Magic Flute* [Bryn
Mawr, Pa.: O. Ditson, 1888], quoted in Susan A. Blain, ed.
Imaging the Word, vol. 2 of Arts and Lectionary Resource
[Cleveland: United Church Press, 1995], p. 141)

BENEDICTION

When Jesus' glory is revealed to us,
   we become transformed.
We are not who we were before.
Go now to your homes, your neighborhoods,
   your schools, and places of work as new people.
Go as Christians illumined by the glory of God in Christ.
Be renewed and be radiant.

VISUAL AND DRAMATIC SUGGESTIONS

Throughout the service pairs of people could portray
transformation. This would occur unannounced, at various preplanned points throughout the service. With
two large screens overlapping to create a path to exit in
the center (dark fabric over a PVC pipe frame could
work) the following pairs could image transformation:
   From the left, a limping man with a cane walks
   halfway across the altar then disappears behind the

screen. From behind, he reenters, without the cane, skipping or dancing.

Same sequence; a woman enters with a large water bottle, disappears, and then reenters with a bottle of wine.

A young girl enters, carrying a ukulele, and disappears behind the screen. Then from behind, continuing across, a woman enters, carrying a guitar.

Two children enter, fighting with toy swords (portraying an Israeli and a Palestinian). They reenter as friends, arms around each other's shoulder.

Other pairs: Old person transition to young, someone carrying a heavy burden reenters without the load.

FEBRUARY 9, 2005

Ash Wednesday
Rebecca Gaudino

COLOR
Purple or Gray

SCRIPTURE READINGS
Joel 2:1-2, 12-17; Psalm 51:1-17; 2 Corinthians 5:20*b*–6:10;
Matthew 6:1-6, 16-21

THEME IDEAS
Ash Wednesday's scriptures are all set in times of
upheaval—upheaval in the world, like the locust army
about to decimate the crops of Joel's Judah; upheaval in our
personal lives, like the calamities threatening Paul or our
complicity in what causes pain around us. Each reading
calls us to seek God in a deep and authentic way that yields
healing and hope. And if we truly seek God, the fearful
"day of the LORD" (Joel) becomes the "day of salvation"
(2 Corinthians) in which we discover the courage and
strength to be coworkers with God and to bring hope to all.

CALL TO WORSHIP (JOEL 2)
[Include the blowing of a trumpet or shofar.]

Voice 1   Blow the trumpet in Zion;
                 sound the alarm on my holy mountain!
                 Let all the inhabitants of the land tremble,
                 for the day of the LORD is coming, it
                 is near—

Voice 2	Blow the trumpet in Zion; sanctify a fast; call a solemn assembly; gather the people— the aged, the children, the bridegroom, the bride. Sanctify the congregation!
Voice 1	Between the vestibule and the altar let the priests, the ministers of the LORD, weep. Let them say,
Pastor(s)	"Spare your people, O LORD, and do not make your heritage a mockery, a byword among the nations. Why should it be said among the peoples, 'Where is their God?' "
Voices 1 & 2	Blow the trumpet in Zion! Gather the people! Sanctify the congregation!

CALL TO WORSHIP (JOEL 2, 2 CORINTHIANS 5, PSALM 51)

The day of the LORD is near—
a day of darkness and gloom,
a day of clouds and thick darkness!
Yet even now, says the LORD,
return to me with all your heart,
with fasting, with weeping, and with mourning;
rend your hearts and not your clothing.
Be reconciled to God!
The sacrifice acceptable to God is a broken spirit,
a broken and contrite heart.

CONTEMPORARY GATHERING WORDS (JOEL 2, 2 CORINTHIANS 5, PSALM 51)

The world around us is upside down—
wars, droughts, wrongful imprisonments, riots, hunger!

**Our own lives are often upside down—
afflictions, hardships, sleepless nights,
transgressions!**
We know that our world is broken.
We know that we are broken.
God calls out, "Return to me, return to me
with all your heart!"
**We gather before you and call out to you,
"Have mercy on us and on our world, O God.
Have mercy on us!"**

CONTEMPORARY GATHERING WORDS (JOEL 2, PSALM 51)

Even on this day of clouds and thick darkness,
this day of alarm and gloom, even now, God calls out,
"Return to me with all your heart,
with fasting, with weeping, and with mourning."
**We weep for our broken world
and for our own brokenness.
Restore to us the joy of your salvation!**

OPENING PRAYER (PSALM 51)

O God, passionately righteous and just,
we are not always righteous and just.
Do not cast us away from your presence.
We bring to you broken and contrite hearts.
O God, steadfastly loving and merciful,
accept our worship and have mercy on us. Amen.

COLLECT (2 CORINTHIANS 5, PSALM 51, MATTHEW 6)

Jesus, Sinless Christ, Savior, Brother,
who identified with us
and knew the upheaval and deathliness of sin,
we call out for new and right spirits.
We long for healing and wholeness,

through the love and mercy of our God
who sees all in secret,
through the power of the Spirit,
who dwells within and renews all. Amen.

BENEDICTION (JOEL 2, PSALM 51, 2 CORINTHIANS 5)

"The day of the Lord is near! Rend your hearts!"
Hearing news of alarm and gloom,
we come before God.
We offer broken hearts.
We call out for restoration.
Hear the glad news, "Now is the acceptable time...
the day of salvation!"
O God, you have restored in us
the joy of our salvation.
Hear our gladness and praise!
Let us not accept the grace of God in vain.
We will work together with God
to share the joy of our salvation with all.
Hear our gladness and praise!

FEBRUARY 13, 2005

First Sunday in Lent
Robert Blezard

COLOR
Purple

SCRIPTURE READINGS
Genesis 2:15-17; 3:1-7; Psalm 32; Romans 5:12-19; Matthew 4:1-11

THEME IDEAS
We are willful creatures born of a fallen humanity. From the very beginning, we have been easily seduced by sin, disregarding God's benevolent instructions and listening instead to those who speak half-truths, with promises of fulfillment that ultimately lead to our own destruction. Blindly following our desires and reaching for the shiny treasures that catch our eye, we live in death apart from God. We are saved from spiritual suicide only by the grace of God that extends forgiveness and justification to all who confess their sin, turn to God, and walk in new ways of life through Jesus the Christ.

CALL TO WORSHIP (PSALM 32)
We keep silent in our sinfulness.
Our bodies waste away.
God's hand is heavy upon us.
Our strength is dried up.

We call to God in our distress,
God delivers and preserves us.
We confess our sins to God.
God forgives and loves us.
Be glad in God and rejoice!
We shout for joy!

CALL TO WORSHIP (PSALM 32, ROMANS 5)

Sin brings us to death's dominion.
Our souls cry out to God.
Disobedience is our legacy.
Our souls cry out to God.
We are powerless to free ourselves.
Our souls cry out to God.
We beg for mercy and grace.
Our souls cry out to God.
We turn to Jesus the Christ, who saves us.
Our souls cry out to God.
We long for God's abundant gift of grace.
Our souls cry out to God.
In Christ, we are justified and made righteous.
Our souls give thanks to God.

CONTEMPORARY GATHERING WORDS (PSALM 32, ROMANS 5)

Hear us, O God! We are a fallen race:
disobedient, headstrong, and greedy.
Only God's grace will save us.
We are driven by our insatiable hungers
and unquenchable desires.
Only God's grace will save us.
Defeated by our sin, we turn to God.
Hear our prayer!
Only God's grace will save us.
Jesus the Christ will scrub the stain of sin from our souls.
Only God's grace will save us.
Christ revives us with abundant mercy and new life.
Only God's grace has saved us.

PRAISE SENTENCES (PSALM 32, ROMANS 5)

O God, like a thunderstorm in the desert,
    your grace restores our parched souls.
We are redeemed not because we are good,
    but because you are merciful.
We rejoice in the saving power of Jesus the Christ,
    who delivers us from the death of sin.

OPENING PRAYER (PSALM 32, ROMANS 5)

Draw near to us, O God!
Help us, for we have need of you!
Left on our own,
    we wither and die in our sin
        like a tree without water.
But we have hope in you, O God.
Your love and mercy flow abundantly
    and freely to all.
From the very roots of our souls,
    your love through Christ Jesus
        waters and sustains us.
Our lives will bud and blossom with your life,
    and in your time bear fruit. Amen.

PRAYER OF CONFESSION (GENESIS 3)

God of mercy, from the time of Adam and Eve,
    we have been a sinful and self-centered race.
We come to you with our faults and fears,
    our shortcomings and our sin.
Hear our prayer and forgive us.
Wipe our tears of sadness away with your love.
Help us to receive grace and newness of life
    through your son, Jesus, our Lord. Amen.

PRAYER OF CONFESSION (GENESIS 3, ROMANS 5)

O merciful God,
    you created the world in perfect order,

granting us all we need to live in joy and happiness.
In our sin, we turned away from you,
  losing our way and despoiling your creation.
Chasing after our petty needs and our needy pettiness,
  we focus our hearts on ourselves instead of you.
Blinded by our self-centeredness,
  we fail to see the injustice we perpetuate,
  we fail to see the needy at our doorstep,
  we fail to see the degradation we wreak,
  and we even fail to see just how much we fail to see.
In your mercy, O God,
  pour your grace upon us,
  bring us to new life,
    that we may see and respond. Amen.

BENEDICTION (PSALM 32)
From the bondage of sin, we are free!
  May God's renewing grace sustain us!
God has brought us from death to life!
  May God's renewing grace sustain us!
We will walk in faith and victory.
  May God's renewing grace sustain us!
We will live the good news of God's deliverance.
  May God's renewing grace sustain us!

BENEDICTION (ROMANS 5)
From sin's deep despair, God's hand has lifted us.
God has freely given us the grace that brings new life.
Let us go forth in boldness, confidence, and strength.
Amen.

BENEDICTION
Go in peace!
  God's mercy is great.
Go in peace!
  God's love is endless.
Go in peace!
  God's grace abounds.

FEBRUARY 20, 2005

Second Sunday in Lent
Mary Petrina Boyd

COLOR

Purple

SCRIPTURE READINGS

Genesis 12:1-4*a*; Psalm 121; Romans 4:1-5, 13-17; John 3:1-17

THEME IDEAS

People often associate Lent with dismal liturgies of penitence. Interestingly, however, Lent means spring, and these lessons remind us of the promise of new life and new possibilities. As the bulbs break through the soil, so God works newness in the midst of our despair. If we focus too closely on our human failings, we lose sight of what is truly important: God's goodness, God's promise, and God's blessing. God calls to us, leading us into new adventures of faith. God's love and faithfulness are never ending, and we are invited to respond in faith. Faced with the ultimate questions of life and death, we hear God's words of truth and love.

CALL TO WORSHIP (GENESIS 12, PSALM 121)

Come on a journey, a journey of faith!
Leave what is familiar and see where God will lead.
Put your trust in God, who is our help.
Worship the Creator of heaven and earth.

CALL TO WORSHIP (PSALM 121)

I lift up my eyes to the hills—
from where will my help come?
My help comes from the LORD,
who made heaven and earth.
God will not let your foot be moved,
the One who keeps you will not slumber....
The LORD will keep you from all evil;
God will keep your life.
The LORD will keep your going out and your coming in
from this time on and forevermore.

CONTEMPORARY GATHERING WORDS (GENESIS 12, ROMANS 4)

Come and follow God, and you will find promise.
We worship a God of promise.
Come on a journey of faith, and you will find grace.
We worship a God of grace.
Go where God calls, and you will find blessing.
We worship a God of blessing.

CONTEMPORARY GATHERING WORDS

As the rain feeds the thirsty earth,
God keeps us in hope.
As the bud springs forth from tender shoots,
God keeps us in faith.
As the flower begins to bloom,
God keeps us in love.

PRAISE SENTENCES (GENESIS 12)

God will call us into new adventures!
God promises blessings and life abundant!

PRAISE SENTENCES (PSALM 121)

God is our help and our strength!
The Creator of the heavens and the earth cares for us!
God watches over us. We need not fear!

PRAISE SENTENCES (JOHN 3)

God so loved the world that God gave Jesus to us!
In Jesus Christ, God offers the gift of eternal life!
God gives birth to new life in the midst of death!

OPENING PRAYER (GENESIS 12, JOHN 3)

God of the ages,
    you call your people into new pilgrimages of faith.
We are so often fearful and reluctant
    to start something new.
We don't want to leave what is comfortable.
Give us brave and faithful hearts,
    that we may trust in your promise
        of unending love and care. Amen.

OPENING PRAYER (PSALM 121, JOHN 3)

God of heaven and earth,
    you have created us, you care for us,
    and you redeem us.
When we wonder how we can go on,
    you remind us that you watch over us
    and neither slumber nor sleep.
When questions fill our minds,
    and we do not know where to turn,
    you help us to remember
        that God loves the world.
May we trust in your promises,
    serving you with joy. Amen.

PRAYER OF CONFESSION (GENESIS 12, JOHN 3)

O Lord, sometime we come to you in the night,
    afraid of what others might think.
Sometimes, when you invite us to begin journeys of faith,
    we refuse.
We hear your promises,
    but we are filled with doubts,

unsure about our future.
Give us courage, beckoning God,
   to answer your call
      and become a blessing to the world.
May the promise of eternal life
   make us bold and daring in this life,
   so that we live by grace alone. Amen.

PRAYER OF CONFESSION (GENESIS 12, ROMANS 4, JOHN 3)

We come, bringing the dead and empty places
of our lives.
   God gives life to the dead.
We do not know what to do.
We cannot find the answers we seek.
   God creates order out of chaos.
We feel unloved. We are sure that no one cares.
   **God so loved the world
   that God gave us Jesus Christ.**
We are afraid of life. We are afraid of death.
   **Those who believe in Jesus shall not perish,
   but have eternal life.**
Lord, forgive our doubts and our fears.
   Help us to rejoice in your blessings.

BENEDICTION (GENESIS 12, ROMANS 4)

God is calling us to follow.
   May we find the faith to answer that call.
God has blessed us, now and forever.
   May we be a blessing to the world.

BENEDICTION (GENESIS 12, PSALM 121, JOHN 3)

The LORD will keep / your going out and your coming in
   from this time on and forevermore.
Go in peace, knowing that God's blessings are abundant
   and that God loves you.

FEBRUARY 27, 2005

Third Sunday in Lent
Christine S. Boardman

COLOR
Purple

SCRIPTURE READINGS
Exodus 17:1-7; Psalm 95; Romans 5:1-11; John 4:5-42

THEME IDEAS
Water is a basic element that all living things need to survive. Some experts, ranging from global politicians to local environmentalists, claim that, in this century, water will be an issue of major concern. If wars are waged, the scarcity of water may cause untold hardship and tragedy. Most of us can identify with the personal experiences of fear and thirst. God in Jesus Christ offers us a basic relationship of love and trust as disciples. We meet this relationship in the wilderness of our lives and in the cup that we offer to others who also need the basics to live. On this Lenten journey, may we be less "testy" and more grateful for all that God has done and will do.

CALL TO WORSHIP (EXODUS 17)
People of God, seek here what you need to live.
We seek God's presence as we journey.
People of God, receive the life of Christ
in this communion.

We receive the spiritual refreshment we seek.
People of God, accept God's blessings
and seek to offer yourselves in service.
**We accept our blessings and willingly share them
with others.**
People of God, test less and trust more.
**As we gather for worship, may we seek, receive,
accept, and share the good news in Jesus Christ.**

CALL TO WORSHIP (PSALM 95)

Let us sing to God a joyful song.
Let us sing of good news and hopeful belonging.
Let us leave behind our need of signs and proof.
Let us be receptive to the new life God creates.
Let us rejoice because the God of grace has found us.
Let us worship and praise God.

CONTEMPORARY GATHERING WORDS (ROMANS 5)

Brothers and sisters in Christ, let us bask in God's grace.
Let us luxuriate in the peace we know as forgiven people.
Pour out your Holy Spirit!
Let us practice our faith and grow strong in our witness.
Pour out your Holy Spirit!
There is peace to calm our lives.
Pour out your Holy Spirit!
Let us be ministers of reconciliation
in the name of our Sovereign Jesus Christ.
Pour out your Holy Spirit!

PRAISE SENTENCES (ROMANS 5)

Come to worship and rejoice in our hope.
Worship God! Hope in God!
Come to worship and rejoice in our hope.
Worship God! Hope in God!
Come to worship and rejoice in our hope.
Worship God! Hope in God!

OPENING PRAYER

Holy God of life-giving water,
> we come to worship, aware of our thirst for meaning
>> in a dueling world.

Hear us as we sing songs of praise
> and as we speak words of confession.

Receive our gratitude for your presence
> of grace and hope.

Visit us at the well of our desire and desperation.
Let us hear again your offer of peace to this world.
We worship in the name of Jesus, the Christ. Amen.

PRAYER OF CONFESSION

God of glory and of steadfast gifts,
> continue to bless us as we gather.

On our Lenten journey of grievance and discovery,
> we acknowledge our loneliness.

Be with us now,
> not as a demand we make
> but as a need we confess.

Open us to hear your word of comfort and belonging.
Free us to express our pain and our pleasure
> as your people—
>> a people called and claimed in your steadfast love.

Open each one here
> to listen for your offer of grace, peace, and love.

When we fear the cost of discipleship,
> forgive us.

When we hide our discontent and our feeble attempts
> to witness to your call to redemption,
>> forgive us.

Cleanse us now of what we would try to hide from you.
Give us what we need to follow Jesus with renewed zeal.
May we take what you offer
> and proclaim to others

what you have done in Jesus Christ,
our Sovereign and our Savior. Amen.

BENEDICTION

Go in peace. Go in love. Go to witness. Go with God.
May the Holy Spirit continue to pour living water on us.
May we be blessed and empowered
to tell our stories of faith, in the name of our Sovereign
Jesus Christ. Amen.

BENEDICTION

We have gathered to offer God thanks and praise.
   Bless us as we scatter to tell our stories of faith.
We have gathered to receive God's gift of grace.
   Bless us as we proclaim what God has done for us.
Let us leave as hopeful people ready to share
the new life Christ brings. Alleluia.
   Alleluia.
Amen.
   Amen.

MARCH 6, 2005

Fourth Sunday in Lent/One Great Hour of Sharing

Mary J. Scifres

COLOR
Purple

SCRIPTURE READINGS
1 Samuel 16:1-13; Psalm 23; Ephesians 5:8-14; John 9:1-41

THEME IDEAS
In John's Gospel, Jesus says, "I came into this world . . . so that those who do not see may see, and those who do see may become blind." Throughout these scriptures, secrets are unveiled as light overcomes darkness and God opens the eyes of the blind.

CALL TO WORSHIP (1 SAMUEL 16)
Let us come peaceably, offering ourselves
in sacrifice to God.
We bring ourselves, our lives,
our gifts into this holy place.
Let us come with open eyes and open hearts,
waiting for the revelation of God.
We bring our hearts and minds, our hopes
and dreams into this holy place.
Come into this holy place, for God is with us.
Thanks be to God!

CALL TO WORSHIP (EPHESIANS 5)

Sleepers, awake!
But we are weary from the journey.
Sleepers, arise!
But death is all around.
Sleepers, walk into the light!
The light of Christ calls.
Children, behold, Christ is with us!
The light of Christ leads.
Friends, rejoice, for we are the children of light!
As children of God, we come into this place.
Let us walk in the light of Christ.

CONTEMPORARY GATHERING WORDS (EPHESIANS 5, JOHN 9)

Once we walked in darkness,
but Christ calls us into the light.
Glory to God!
Once we stumbled from blindness,
but God offers guidance for our journey.
Glory to God!
Once we slept as if dead,
but the Spirit fills us with new life.
Glory to God!
Glory indeed, for we are the children of God!

PRAISE SENTENCES (EPHESIANS 5)

Jesus is the light of the world.
Jesus is the light of the world!
Come, walk in the light of Christ Jesus.
Jesus is the light of the world!
Come, live in the light of God.
Jesus is the light of the world!

OPENING PRAYER (PSALM 23, JOHN 9)

Shepherd God,
be with us on this day and always.

Guide our steps,
    that we might not stumble.
Open our eyes,
    that we might see your glory.
Warm our hearts,
    that we might feel your love.
Bless our worship,
    that we might glorify your name.
Amen.

PRAYER (PSALM 23)

Loving God,
    you are our shepherd and our guide.
In your care,
    we have all that we need.
When we are tired,
    you give us rest.
When we are thirsty,
    you fill us to overflowing.
When our souls are weary,
    you renew us with your Spirit.
You guide our steps,
    that we might walk in holiness with you.
Even when we walk through the deepest valleys,
    we need not be afraid,
    for you are with us.
Your strength and your might,
    your light and love,
    they comfort me.
Surely your goodness and mercy will follow us
    all the days of our lives.
And we shall dwell in your house forever. Amen.

PRAYER OF CONFESSION (EPHESIANS 5)

God of light and love,
    we are sometimes drawn to the darkness.
Surround us with your light,

that we might walk in your ways
and live in your love.
In Christ's name, we pray. Amen.

WORDS OF ASSURANCE (PSALM 23, EPHESIANS 5)

Once we were in darkness, but now,
through the grace of Christ, we walk in the light.
Goodness and mercy are all around, for God is with us.
Through God's grace,
we will dwell in the house of the Lord forever!

PRAYER OF CONFESSION (1 SAMUEL 16)

Forgive us, gracious God,
for seeing only what lies on the surface of things.
Help us to look deeply, as Christ looked,
that we might see your ways and your will.

WORDS OF ASSURANCE (1 SAMUEL 16)

Do not look on the appearance,
for God does not see as humans see.
Look to the heart, for in doing so,
our eyes will be opened and we will see as Christ sees.
Then, we will be the children of light.

BENEDICTION (EPHESIANS 5)

In Christ Jesus, you are light.
We go now to shine into a world of darkness.
Live in the light.
We will walk with the Lord!

BENEDICTION (PSALM 23)

Walk with confidence and faith as you leave this place,
for the Lord is your shepherd and your guide.
Goodness and mercy will follow you
as you walk this path with God.
Go in peace.

MARCH 13, 2005

Fifth Sunday in Lent
B. J. Beu

COLOR
Purple

SCRIPTURE READINGS
Ezekiel 37:1-14; Psalm 130; Romans 8:6-11; John 11:1-45

THEME IDEAS
From the valley filled with dry bones in Ezekiel, to the death of Lazarus in John, this theme focuses on experiences of loss and death and the hope of new life in God. We feel dried up, devoid of breath, aching from the loss of loved ones, but death and loss do not have the final word. We worship a God who brings new life and new visions. We place our hope in a God who has power even over death. What have we to fear? With Paul, we know that: "To set the mind on the flesh is death, but to set the mind on the Spirit is life and peace" (Romans 8:6). Lent is a time to choose life.

CALL TO WORSHIP (EZEKIEL 37)
Behold a miracle!
God has clothed our dry bones with flesh.
Behold a miracle!
God has breathed into us new life that we might live.
Behold a miracle!

The graves are opened. Death has lost its sting.
Come let us worship the One who never forsakes us.
Let us worship the Lord.

CALL TO WORSHIP (PSALM 130)

Let our souls wait for the Lord,
more than those who wait for the morning,
more than those who wait for the morning.
Put your hope in the Lord!
We put our hopes in God's steadfast love.
God has great power to redeem our lives.
We turn to God,
who redeems us from all our iniquities.

CONTEMPORARY GATHERING WORDS (JOHN 11)

God is life!
But death runs swift.
Believe in the Resurrection!
But death seems more certain.
Christ is the resurrection and the life!
We want to believe.
Those who live and believe in Christ will never die.
We have come to find faith in the Lord of life!

PRAISE SENTENCES (JOHN 11)

Praise the Lord of life!
Praise the One who brings us back from the grave!
In Christ we will never truly die.
Praise the Lord of Life!

OPENING PRAYER (EZEKIEL 37)

God of promise and hope,
we come to you feeling dried up,
like a valley filled with dry bones.
Share your visions of new life with us,
that we might have hope for our future.

Bring us up from the grave,
   that we might live as people of promise.
Put your Spirit within us,
   that we might have life everlasting.
Amen.

OPENING PRAYER (ROMANS 8)

Holy God,
   you sent your Son into the world,
   that we might set our minds on life and peace,
   rather than on the things of the flesh.
May the Spirit who raised Christ from the dead
   bring us fullness of life,
   that we might live according to your holy laws
      and be a source of light in a world
         that has learned to love the darkness. Amen.

PRAYER OF CONFESSION (JOHN 11)

Lord of life,
   we come to you consumed by our worry and our pain.
We too often blame you for not being there in our need,
   rather than turning to you for help in moments of loss.
Help us put our faith in your promise of healing and life.
Teach us anew that you are the resurrection and the life.
Help us remember that you weep when we weep,
   and seek to lead us to newness of life,
   through Jesus Christ our Lord. Amen.

ASSURANCE OF PARDON (EZEKIEL 37)

God makes us a promise:
   "I will put my spirit within you, and you shall live."
The God who showed Ezekiel
   that a valley of dry bones could live again,
   will bring us to newness of life through Christ,
   who is the resurrection and the life.

BENEDICTION (PSALM 130)

Go with the blessings of the One who forgives our sins.
We go with God's blessings!
Go with the blessings of the One who redeems us.
We go with God's blessings!
Go with the blessings of God.
We go with God's blessings!

MARCH 20, 2005

Passion/Palm Sunday

Brian Wren

COLOR
Purple

PALM SUNDAY READINGS
Psalm 118:1-2, 19-29; Matthew 21:1-11

PASSION SUNDAY READINGS
Isaiah 50:4-9*a*; Psalm 31:9-16; Philippians 2:5-11; Matthew 26:14–27:66

THEME IDEAS (PALM SUNDAY)
By quoting Zechariah and omitting his reference to triumph and victory, Matthew highlights Jesus' entry into Jerusalem as a challenge to the paraphernalia of coercion. Ambling along on a donkey, Jesus satirizes generals on warhorses, nonverbally proclaiming that God intends to "cut off the chariot from Ephraim/and the war horse from Jerusalem" (Zechariah 9:10). Psalm 118:19-23 can be read as joining Palm Sunday (the city gates) with Good Friday (the stone rejected) and Easter (opening the gates of death).

THEME IDEAS (PASSION SUNDAY)
The challenge is to tell Matthew's story as compellingly in today's visual culture as in the aural and oral culture

of fourth-century Jerusalem, when people wept as the story was declaimed.

CALL TO WORSHIP (MATTHEW 21)

Still Jesus comes:
to us, to our town,
to our nation, to our world.
Ride on, ride on in majesty!
Still Jesus rides:
to peace rejected, trust betrayed,
and hope destroyed.
If we are silent, the stones will cry aloud.
Still Jesus calls:
"Come with me, all the way."
Blessed is the One who comes
in the name of the Living God.
Hosanna in the highest!

CALL TO WORSHIP (PHILIPPIANS 2, MATTHEW 21)

On this day, imagine:
a city on a hilltop,
a hot, dusty road,
and a man sitting on a donkey,
riding through cheering crowds and frowning priests.
This is the prophet Jesus
from Nazareth in Galilee!
On this day, imagine:
a table in an upstairs room,
voices in the night among olive trees,
a shackled prisoner, bleeding and bruised,
and three gaunt crosses on a skull-shaped hill.
This is Christ Jesus
who took the form of a slave
and died to bring us to God.
God be praised! Amen!

CONTEMPORARY GATHERING WORDS (PALM SUNDAY)

Jesus is coming to Jerusalem.
Ask him what he is doing:
Why are you riding a donkey?
Where are your chariots and armies?
What can you possibly achieve
with pilgrims waving branches?
What are you doing, and why?

CONTEMPORARY GATHERING WORDS (PASSION SUNDAY)

Follow Jesus slowly; follow at a donkey's pace.
Do not run past Friday
and speed to Easter Sunday.
(Then either this):
Follow to the Temple. Follow to the upper room.
Follow to the garden. Follow to the judgment hall.
Follow through the city gate. Follow to the cross.
(or this):
Climb the steps to the Temple court.
Watch the meal in the upper room.
Hide among trees in the garden.
Stand outside the judgment hall.
Stumble to the hilltop.
Crouch beneath the cross.

PRAISE SENTENCES

Donkey-riding Savior,
waving palms, we praise you!
With courage now you come,
knowing you will be betrayed,
knowing you will suffer, naked on a cross.
Waving palms, we praise you,
by entering your story,
and walking with you on your way. Amen.

PRAISE SENTENCES (ISAIAH 50, PHILIPPIANS 2)
Hail, King Jesus!
Your steadfast love endures forever.
You gave your back to those who struck you.
Your steadfast love endures forever.
You did not hide your face
from insult and spitting.
Your steadfast love endures forever.
For us, and for our salvation,
you followed the way of God
to the point of death, even death on a cross.
Your steadfast love endures forever.
We praise you, Name above all names!
Your steadfast love endures forever.

OPENING PRAYER
Living Christ,
always you approach our gates,
not in a tank
but on a bicycle.
Always you die for us,
not robed in dignity, or full of years,
but too young, too soon,
naked, shamed, and tortured.
Silently, in wonder,
we praise you and adore you.
(silence)
With heart and body, mind and strength,
we praise you, we adore you, we love you. Amen.

OPENING PRAYER
Holy God, you know who we are,
and where we are, in the story we tell today.
Are we following Jesus, more or less?
Are we eating with him, yet betraying his trust?
Are we embarrassed, afraid to admit we know him?

Are we running away, or watching from a distance?
Holy God, you know where we are.
Find us in Christ's story.
Show us your love for us, our love for you,
and our longing to love you more,
through Jesus Christ. Amen.

BENEDICTION

Remember, this week,
how Jesus came to Jerusalem,
what he did,
what he refused to do,
and what was done to him.
Live within his story.
Let it feed your spirit,
stretch your mind,
fill your imagination,
and warm your heart,
to the glory of God. Amen.

BENEDICTION

Go, giving thanks
that Jesus did not raise an army,
draw a sword,
or run away to safety.
Go, giving thanks
that Jesus trod the path of peaceful love
to its bitter, glorious end.
Go in the strength of the Three who are One:
sent by the Sender,
moved by the Spirit,
and guided by Christ, crucified and risen. Amen.

Copyright © 2003 by Brian Wren

MARCH 24, 2005

Holy Thursday

B. J. Beu and Mary J. Scifres

COLOR

Purple

SCRIPTURE READINGS

Exodus 12:1-4 (5-10), 11-14; Psalm 116:1-2, 12-19;
1 Corinthians 11:23-26; John 13:1-17, 31*b*-35

THEME IDEAS

God's deliverance is the central theme of today's scripture readings, as the church recalls the night Jesus washed the feet of his disciples and celebrated the Passover feast with them one last time. The same God who passed over the homes of the Hebrews in Egypt, sparing the Israelites from the plague of death, is present in the church's sacrament of Holy Communion, as we are made whole through the sharing of Christ's body and blood. Psalm 116 expresses the joy felt by God's people as we are redeemed in our hour of need.

CALL TO WORSHIP (PSALM 116)

The snares of death surround us.
   We will call on the name of the Lord and be saved!
The pangs of distress and anguish encompass us.
   We will call on the name of the Lord and be saved!
The bonds of despair lay hold of us.
   We will call on the name of the Lord and be saved!

CALL TO WORSHIP OR INVITATION TO COMMUNION (1 CORINTHIANS 11)
Come, all you who are broken,
and eat of the bread of life,
which makes us whole.
We are made whole
as we eat from the bread of life.
Come, all you who thirst for God's salvation,
and drink from the cup of heaven.
We are made one with God
as we drink from the cup of heaven.
Come let us eat at Christ's table
in anticipation of the heavenly banquet
that we will share with all God's people.
Taste and see that the Lord is good.

CONTEMPORARY GATHERING WORDS (JOHN 13)
We come with hands that have worked
and feet that are tired.
We come to Christ,
who promises to wash us clean.
Come into the presence of our loving God,
the One who serves us still.

CONTEMPORARY GATHERING WORDS (EXODUS 12; 1 CORINTHIANS 11)
This is a day of remembrance,
a day to celebrate God's faithfulness.
This we do in remembrance of Christ.
This is a night of repentance,
a night to mourn our lack of faithfulness.
This we do in remembrance of Christ.
This is a week of holiness,
a time to walk in the ways of God.
This we do in remembrance of Christ.
In remembrance, in repentance, in search of holiness,

we come before the Lord.
This we do in remembrance of Christ.

PRAISE SENTENCES (1 CORINTHIANS 11)

Remember the Lord.
Remember the Lord!
Remember Christ's love.
Remember Christ's love!

PRAISE SENTENCES (JOHN 13)

I will call upon the Lord.
I will call upon the Lord!
I will lift up my voice in praise.
I will lift up my voice in praise!
I will offer up my thanks!
Thanks and praise belong to God!

OPENING PRAYER (PSALM 116)

With love and hope,
    we call upon your name, O God.
We pray for your presence
    in this place and in our lives.
Hear our cries.
Listen to our prayers.
As we enter into this time of worship,
    accept our thanks and gratitude.
Turn our lives into offerings of love and justice.
Create in us clean hearts and joy-filled hope,
    that we might live our praise
    in lives that are pleasing to you.
In your holy name, we pray. Amen.

OPENING PRAYER (JOHN 13)

God of love and service,
    help us to serve one another
        as you first served us.
Grant us the love

that shows others our faith in you.
Bless our time of worship,
 that our praise may glorify your name
  and our lives may reflect your glory.
Amen.

PRAYER OF CONFESSION (1 CORINTHIANS 11)

God of grace and mercy,
 pour out your holiness
  in these gifts of bread and wine.
Wash over us with your forgiveness,
 that our sins may be forgiven
  and our lives redeemed.
Lord have mercy.
Christ have mercy.
Lord have mercy.
Amen.

WORDS OF ASSURANCE (1 CORINTHIANS 11)

This is Christ's body,
 broken for us that we might be whole.
This is the cup of the new covenant,
 proclaiming forgiveness
  for all who call upon God's name.
We, who call upon God's holy name,
 are forgiven through Christ's holiness and grace.

BENEDICTION

See how Christ has loved us.
So now must we love one another.
See how Christ has loved us.
So now must we love the world.

MARCH 25, 2005

Good Friday
Hans Holznagel

COLOR

Black or None

SCRIPTURE READINGS

Isaiah 52:13–53:12; Psalm 22; Hebrews 10:16-25; John 18:1–19:42

THEME IDEAS

Some churches observe Good Friday with a service marking the Stations of the Cross or the "seven last words of Christ." Planners of such services may find components below useful. Those who use the lectionary will also find here the lengthy Fourth Gospel account, beginning in the garden of Jesus' betrayal and ending in the garden of his tomb. The story is divided into nine readings, with congregational responses. No benediction is provided, in keeping with the somber mood of the day of crucifixion and burial. Worshipers may be asked to depart in reflective silence, with worship not ending until the Easter Sunday benediction.

CALL TO WORSHIP

Draw near to holy ground, O people.
Bring the weight of the world.
We bring the weight of our lives.
Bring the weight of your sorrows.

We bring the weight of our lives.
Bring the weight of your desertions and betrayals.
We bring the weight of our lives.
Bring the weight of your accusations and scorns.
We bring the weight of our lives.
Lay your burdens at the foot of the cross.
**For strength and hope,
we come to lay our burdens down.**

Contemporary Gathering Words
Jesus cleansed and fed us last night,
and our hearts leapt with mystery and joy.
His words were strange, but now we remember.
We come to walk the path Christ walked—
from the garden to the court,
from the court to the cross,
and from the cross to the tomb.
We come to see what discipleship costs.
Show us the path, O God.
Show us Jesus and show us ourselves.
Deepen our faith.
Lead on.

Opening Prayer or Call to Worship
The garden calls, O God.
Will we take up the sword again?
The courtyard calls, O God.
Will we hide by the fire again?
The Cross calls, O God.
Will we desert you again?
The garden looms, O God.
Lead on. Teach us as we try again. Amen.

Gospel Reading with Responsives
[With planning, the Gospel may also be presented dramatically, with readers or actors taking on the roles of Jesus, Judas, a narrator, and others.]

Reading 1 (John 18:1-27)
Response 1 (Isaiah 53:6)
**All we like sheep have gone astray;
we have all turned to our own way.**
Reading 2 (John 18:28-32)
Response 2 (Hebrews 10:17)
**The Holy Spirit says, "I will remember their sins
and their lawless deeds no more."**
Reading 3 (John 18:33-38*a*)
Response 3 (Isaiah 53:9*cd*)
**He had done no violence,
and there was no deceit in his mouth.**
Reading 4 (John 18:38*b*-40)
Response 4 (Psalm 22:11)
**Do not be far from me, / for trouble is near
and there is no one to help.**
Reading 5 (John 19:1-3)
Response 5 (Isaiah 53:12)
**Yet he bore the sin of many,
and made intercession for the transgressors.**
Reading 6 (John 19:4-7)
Response 6 (Psalm 22:12*b*-13)
**Strong bulls ... surround me;
they open wide their mouths at me,
like a ravening and roaring lion.**
Reading 7 (John 19:8-11)
Response 7 (Isaiah 53:7)
**Like a sheep that before its shearers is silent,
so he did not open his mouth.**
Reading 8 (John 19:12-16*a*)
Response 8 (Isaiah 53:8*a*)
By a perversion of justice he was taken away.
Reading 9 (John 19:16*b*-42)
Response 9 (Silent reflection)

PRAYER OF CONFESSION (PSALM 22)
O God,
we have forsaken you.

We scorn ourselves.
We feel inhuman.
Our hearts melt.
Our bodies break.
O Lord,
    do not be far away!
Hear our cry, we pray. Amen.

ASSURANCE OF PARDON (PSALM 22)

God is holy and does not shame us.
God cradles us as newborns.
God comes quickly to our aid.
Those who seek shall praise the Lord.
May your hearts live forever! Amen.

MARCH 27, 2005

Easter Sunday

Leonard Sweet, Mary J. Scifres, and B. J. Beu

COLOR
White

SCRIPTURE READINGS
Acts 10:34-43; Psalm 118:1-2, 14-24; Colossians 3:1-4; John 20:1-18 or Matthew 28:1-10

THEME IDEAS
A pastor asked a group of second-grade students, "What did Jesus say right after he came out of the grave?" "I know," exclaimed one little girl. "He said, 'Tah-dah!'" Easter is "Tah-dah!" Sunday, for on this holy morning, God laughed out loud. If Lent is a time for crying instead of laughter, then Easter is Laughter Sunday. The rock and roll music of that empty tomb drowns out all dissonant notes—all chords of despair, all choruses of cruelty, all choirs of evil and madness, especially the "Devil's Note" of death, the Great Pretender. The volume of resurrection laughter is so loud that all other sounds are hushed.

CALL TO WORSHIP (PSALM 118)
God is our strength and might.
God has become our salvation.
God has lifted us up.

God is merciful and loving.
Christ is our cornerstone.
Christ makes us one.
God's Spirit is with us now.
And calls us to this place.
Come to the gate of God.
All are welcome here.

CALL TO WORSHIP

Christ is risen! Rejoice on this holy day!
Nothing could kill his love.
No tomb could contain his spirit.
Jesus is with us now! Rejoice on this holy day!
We worship the Christ of love,
who is the resurrection and the life.

CONTEMPORARY GATHERING IDEA

Play the song "Beautiful Day" by U2 while projecting scenes of the empty tomb from the movie *Jesus* (based on John's Gospel), playing without sound. Make postcard-size handouts of the words to "Beautiful Day" on one side and on the other side print: Resurrection 2005/John 20:1-18.

CONTEMPORARY GATHERING WORDS

Rejoice, for Christ is alive!
Christ is risen indeed!
Rejoice, for Christ is alive!
Christ is risen indeed!

CONTEMPORARY GATHERING WORDS (ISAIAH 43)

"I am about to do a new thing;
now it springs forth,
do you not perceive it?
I will make a way in the wilderness
and rivers in the desert..."

to give drink to my chosen people,
the people whom I formed for myself
so that they might declare my praise."

PRAISE SENTENCES (PSALM 118)

Give thanks to God! God's love endures forever!
Give thanks to God! Christ's love will never end!

PRAISE SENTENCES

Christ is risen! Rejoice and give thanks to God!
Christ is risen! Rejoice and give thanks to God!

OPENING PRAYER (JOHN 20)

Lord God,
walk with us in this time of worship,
as you walked with Mary in the garden.
Whisper our names,
that we might hear your voice.
Show us your grace,
that we might know your love.
Grant us your faith,
that we might believe in your resurrection.
In your name, we pray. Amen.

OPENING PRAYER (COLOSSIANS 3)

We come this morning,
seeking the things of Christ.
We pray to you, O God,
looking for your direction.
Bless our time together,
that our worship may center
on your word of love and hope.
Bless our lives,
that others might see Christ in all that we say and do.
Bless the spirit of our worship,
that we might be children of the Resurrection.
In Christ's name we pray. Amen.

RESPONSIVE PRAYER OF THANKSGIVING (PSALM 118)

Give thanks to the Lord.
We praise our God of love!
Give thanks to the Lord.
For God is truly good!
Give thanks to the Lord.
We praise our God of strength and might.
Give thanks to the Lord.
We praise our God who made this day!

PRAYER OF CONFESSION (COLOSSIANS 3)

Resurrection God,
   forgive us when we so focus on our earthly troubles,
   that we forget to seek your heavenly guidance.
Help us to turn our eyes toward you,
   that our sights may be set on your glorious promise.
Search our hearts and cleanse the wounded places
   that prevent us from setting our minds on Christ.
Heal us and make us whole,
   that we might reveal Christ's glory
      in our thoughts and in our lives. Amen.

WORDS OF ASSURANCE (ACTS 10)

We have this promise:
   Everyone who believes in Jesus the Christ
   receives forgiveness of sins through Christ's holy name.

BENEDICTION (COLOSSIANS 3)

Go forth, seeking the things that are from above.
Set your minds on Christ Jesus and God's love.
Live your lives with resurrection hope,
   that all may find love and joy in your presence.

BENEDICTION

Christ is risen! Sing it aloud!
Christ is risen! The Lord is risen indeed!

APRIL 3, 2005

Second Sunday of Easter
B. J. Beu

COLOR
White

SCRIPTURE READINGS
Acts 2:14*a*, 22-32; Psalm 16; 1 Peter 1:3-9; John 20:19-31

THEME IDEAS
Resurrection motifs continue as we hear promises that God will not let death have the final word. The readings in Acts and in Psalm 16 assure us that God does not give the faithful over to the Pit, to languish in Sheol. Therefore, be glad and take heart. Believe the good news of Christ's resurrection and keep the faith, which is more precious than gold. John's Gospel reminds us that faith in the absence of proof leads to blessings. But even if we have doubts, we should be prepared to proclaim with Thomas: "My Lord and my God!" (John 20:28).

CALL TO WORSHIP (PSALM 16)
O God, you are our chosen portion,
the cup of our salvation.
You lift us up in times of trial,
and give us a goodly heritage.
Rejoice in the Lord.
Our hearts are glad to be God's people.

CALL TO WORSHIP (1 PETER 1)
God's mercy has called us here.
God's mercy leads us into life.
The Lord has given us a new birth into a living hope—
hope through the resurrection of Jesus.
The Lord offers us an inheritance that is imperishable,
undefiled, and unfading.
**The power of God protects us
and leads us to our salvation.**
Believe in Christ and rejoice with an indescribable joy.
**We rejoice in faith and proclaim our love for God
who has redeemed us.**

CONTEMPORARY GATHERING WORDS (JOHN 20)
Have you not seen? Have you known?
Christ is risen from the grave!
Have you not seen? Have you known?
Christ has brought us the Holy Spirit!
Have you not seen? Have you known?
Christ is here in our midst to bring us eternal life.

PRAISE SENTENCES
Rejoice in the Lord. God is our hope and our salvation.
Christ is risen. Shout with songs of praise.
Rejoice in the Lord.

OPENING PRAYER (JOHN 20)
Eternal God,
    when the doors of our hearts are shut because of fear,
    be present to us and bless us with your Holy Spirit.
Eternal Christ,
    show us the marks of the holes in your hands and feet,
    that we might cast aside our doubts
        and proclaim with Thomas,
        "My Lord and my God!" Amen.

OPENING PRAYER

God of birth and rebirth we remember
when our souls were pushed from your nest,
how we took flight with the wings of your spirit.
> **But when we stand in line at the bank,**
> **or sit at a red light in traffic, or clean up spills,**
> **or take out the garbage,**
> **we don't feel like soaring eagles.**

We feel like earthbound birds in the dry desert
who long to take to the air.
> **Our wings are caked with dirt,**
> **they are stuck together with grime.**

God of earth, send us resurrection rain.
> **God of love, take your hands**
> **and separate our feathers.**

Show us the brightness of our Color.
Brush our ruffled feathers; feed our souls with your care.
> **Raise us up and let us know your strength**
> **as we take flight once more.**

(Crystal Sygeel)

PRAYER OF CONFESSION (JOHN 20)

God of action, we have great intentions.
> **We have been meaning to call our friends,**
> **meaning to visit our relatives,**
> **meaning to know you better, Lord.**

But intentions without action are empty.
> **Lord, we believe we can be the people**
> **you have called us to be, but only to a point.**

We fall short.
> **We don't show up.**

We forget.
> **Lord, we believe. Help our unbelief.**
> **Turn our good intentions into Easter dances**
> **of commitment and action.**

(Crystal Sygeel)

ASSURANCE OF PARDON (1 PETER 1)

The God who raised Christ from the grave
has offered us an inheritance that is imperishable,
undefiled, and unfading.
Hold fast to your faith,
which is far more precious than gold,
and rejoice in God's salvation.

BENEDICTION (1 PETER 1)

God has blessed us with an eternal inheritance
through Jesus Christ our Lord.
Go forth with faith—
faith that is far more precious than gold—
and be a blessing to all those you meet.

BENEDICTION

Christ, who could not be contained by the grave,
has brought us newness of life.
Christ, who was raised from the dead,
has given us the gift of the Holy Spirit.
Go forth in hope and joy.
We go forth with the blessings of God.

APRIL 10, 2005

Third Sunday of Easter
Bill Hoppe

COLOR
White

SCRIPTURE READINGS
Acts 2:14*a*, 36-41; Psalm 116:1-4, 12-19; 1 Peter 1:17-23; Luke 24:13-35

THEME IDEAS
In the lesson from Acts, Peter speaks of the resurrection of Jesus with such power that some 3,000 people are numbered among the first Christians. Forgiveness of sins and the presence of the Holy Spirit are amazing gifts offered to all who hear the Lord's call. In Luke's Gospel, we find the risen Jesus unfolding scripture to two disciples as they journey to the village of Emmaus. Only when "their eyes were opened" did they truly understand who he was and what he had said. With the miracle of Easter still fresh in our memory, let us be filled with passion and conviction like Peter, proclaiming the good news of Jesus Christ, our risen Lord and Savior!

CALL TO WORSHIP (PSALM 116)
The Lord harkens to our call,
listening to our pleas and hearing our prayers!
We will praise God who gives rest to our souls!
In the courts of the house of the LORD,
in the presence of all God's people,

we acknowledge our faith.
We will call on the Lord as long as we live!
We are your servant, O God;
you have loosed our bonds!
We will offer sacrifices of praise and thanksgiving!
How shall we repay the Lord for all we have been given?
**We will lift up the cup of salvation
and call on the name of the Lord!**

CALL TO WORSHIP

As you walk with us, as we journey together,
Lord, your word fills our hearts!
As you speak with us, as your love is revealed,
Lord, your fire burns in our hearts!
As we proclaim what we have seen and heard,
may all people be drawn to you, the risen Lord!

PRAISE SENTENCES (PSALM 116, ACTS 2)

Jesus is Lord and Messiah!
God's promise is given to us!
The Lord has saved my life!
God has unchained me and set me free!

OPENING PRAYER (1 PETER 1)

Lord, we celebrate the triumph of life over death—
this is the good news of Jesus, our risen savior.
You have ransomed us from our futility—
our salvation wasn't purchased with gold or silver,
or with perishable earthly goods,
but with the precious blood of Christ himself.
In his resurrection, we are born anew with him—
born of the immortal, born of the everlasting,
born into a living hope.
Fill us with all good gifts of your Holy Spirit,
that we may share your love with boldness and power,
with passion and conviction!
In the name of Jesus we pray. Amen.

OPENING PRAYER

Dear Lord, you have so much to show us and to tell us—
    things that no human eyes have seen,
    things that no human ears have heard,
    things that you have prepared for those you love.
Mighty God, your promises are like shelter in a storm—
    to us and to our children,
    to all those far and near,
    to everyone who hears your call.
O, that we might have the mind of Christ,
    that we may know and understand your truth.
We wait as empty vessels,
    ready to be filled to overflowing with your living water,
    as you reveal your love for us through Jesus Christ,
    in whose name we pray. Amen.

PRAYER OF CONFESSION

We're afraid to take a truthful look at ourselves,
yet you see us as we really are.
    Open our eyes, Lord.
Even when we won't listen to you,
you hear us when we call your name.
    Open our ears, Lord.
We keep the light of your word hidden to ourselves,
though you gave it to share with the world.
    Open our mouths, Lord.
May we know and serve the One
who calls us to see, hear, and speak.
    Open our hearts, Lord.

BENEDICTION

Christ has brought us together:
    together in faith, together in hope, together in love.
We have gathered together to be sent out again:
    sent out with the welcome message of God's love!
We go forth together,
    to be living testimonies of Christ's love!

APRIL 17, 2005

Fourth Sunday of Easter
B. J. Beu

COLOR
White

SCRIPTURE READINGS
Acts 2:42-47; Psalm 23; 1 Peter 2:19-25; John 10:1-10

THEME IDEAS
The theme of being sheep in God's flock predominates the day's scriptures. In Psalm 23, we find that God is not only Israel's collective shepherd, God is our individual shepherd. "The LORD is *my* shepherd, *I* shall not want." In Christ, we are God's sheep, and Christ is our shepherd, the guardian of our souls. Because of Christ, we have been given entry into the true gate and been made aware of those who would steal or scatter the sheep for their own purposes. With Christ as our shepherd, we are offered abundant life.

CALL TO WORSHIP (PSALM 23)
The LORD is my shepherd,
I shall not want.
God makes me lie down in green pastures;
God leads me beside still waters;
God restores my soul.
God leads me in right paths....
Surely goodness and mercy shall follow me

all the days of my life,
**and I shall dwell in the house of the LORD my whole
life long.**

CALL TO WORSHIP (1 PETER 2, JOHN 10)

Christ is our shepherd,
the guardian of our souls.
When we go astray,
the shepherd guides us safely home.
Christ opens the gate and calls to us.
We follow the one who calls us by name.
Christ is the true gate.
And we are Christ's flock.

CONTEMPORARY GATHERING WORDS (ACTS 2)

Look! Signs and wonders are done in our midst.
Christ is with us.
Look! Mighty acts of salvation are seen in our midst.
God is with us.
Look! The Spirit of God is blowing through our midst.
The Holy Spirit is with us.

CONTEMPORARY GATHERING WORDS (1 PETER 2, JOHN 10)

Christ is our Shepherd.
We are God's sheep.
Christ is the guardian of our souls.
We hear God's voice.
Christ is leading us into abundant life.
We worship the Shepherd.

PRAISE SENTENCES (PSALM 23)

Christ is our shepherd! Praise God for guiding us!
Christ is our shepherd! Praise God for guiding us!

April 17, 2005

OPENING PRAYER (PSALM 23)

Gentle Shepherd,
    our souls are restless
        until they find their rest in you.
Lead us beside the still waters
    that nurture our souls
        on the living water of your Holy Word.
Save us from the time of trial,
    that we might dwell in your flock
        all the days of our lives.
Be with us as we walk through the dark valleys
    of weakness and fear,
        that we might dwell in your house forever.
Amen.

OPENING PRAYER (JOHN 10)

Loving Christ,
    you are our Shepherd,
        and we are your sheep.
We long to hear your voice
    lead us through the gate of life.
Keep us safe from those
    who seek to steal us from your flock
        like a thief in the night.
Lead us, gentle Shepherd,
    that we might have life,
        and have it abundantly. Amen.

PRAYER OF CONFESSION (ACTS 2)

Eternal God,
    as you kindled the faith of the apostles,
    you are ready to set our souls on fire.
We confess that, given the choice,
    we would choose to keep our possessions,
    than turn over everything to you
        and be transformed.

We would rather trust in our own resourcefulness
than behold the signs and wonders
of living in true Christian community.
Forgive our self-reliance
and replace our calculating nature
with glad and generous hearts.
In Jesus' name we pray. Amen.

ASSURANCE OF PARDON (PSALM 23, JOHN 10)
Christ came that we might have life,
and have it abundantly.
Put your hope and faith in the One
who anoints our head with oil
and makes our cup overflow with God's blessing.

BENEDICTION (ACTS 2)
May your zeal for God set your souls on fire.
Be of good and generous heart,
that all the world may know
you are a disciple of the living Lord.
May the Spirit of God work through you,
that others may be led to believe in the risen Christ.

APRIL 24, 2005

Fifth Sunday of Easter
Laura Jaquith Bartlett

COLOR
White

SCRIPTURE READINGS
Acts 7:55-60; Psalm 31:1-5, 15-16; 1 Peter 2:2-10; John 14:1-14

THEME IDEAS
"Now you are God's people" (1 Peter 2:10). "Do not let your hearts be troubled" (John 14:1). "You know the way to the place where I am going" (John 14:4). These are powerful words of comfort for a congregation that has just heard the story of the stoning of Stephen. Actually, even if you don't read the Acts passage, any congregation that lives in today's world will be longing to hear God's message of mercy. Jesus assures his disciples, and us, that we will not be abandoned and that all we need for salvation we have already, simply by knowing Christ. The glory of God's light radiates from us when we have Christ in our lives.

CALL TO WORSHIP (1 PETER 2)
Once you had not received mercy.
Now we have received mercy.
Once you were not a people.
Now we are God's people!

CALL TO WORSHIP (1 PETER 2, EASTER)

The one who was crucified has been resurrected.
Christ is risen! Alleluia!
The stone which the builders rejected
has become the cornerstone of our faith.
Christ is risen! Alleluia!
God's message of mercy is alive in the world today.
Christ is risen! Alleluia!

CONTEMPORARY GATHERING WORDS (JOHN 14)

Come, you know where we are going.
We follow the footsteps of Jesus, who is the way.
Come, you know the One with whom we go.
We go with Jesus, who is God's Word made flesh.
Come, you know how to be saved.
We go to Jesus, who is our salvation.

PRAISE SENTENCES (PSALM 31)

We praise you, O God. You are a rock of refuge for us.
We praise you, O God. You protect us. You save us.
You love us forever. We praise you, O God.
You are our salvation.

PRAISE SENTENCES (1 PETER 2, *MESSAGE*)

All praise to the One who has chosen us to shine
the light of God's love into the world.
Glory to the One who makes a night-and-day difference
in our lives!
We are precious, chosen by God! Praise be to God!

OPENING PRAYER

God, we come to you with troubled hearts.
Somewhere in the litany of bad-news headlines,
we have forgotten Jesus' words of comfort
and assurance.
We think we have to dig ourselves out of the mess

we have made of your world before we dare
　　to approach you.
Tell us again that you have chosen us to be your people.
Tell us again that we already know you
　　when we receive your son,
　　　　whom you sent into our midst.
Tell us again that all we need is to love Christ,
　　and our lives will radiate your glory into this world,
　　　　a world so desperately in need of your love.
Tell us again, God, tell us again. Amen.

OPENING PRAYER (JOHN 14)

God of glory,
　　we ask that our lives might glorify you.
Help us to see Jesus,
　　that we may also see you.
Help us to know Jesus,
　　that we may also know you.
And help us to love Jesus,
　　that we may also love you.
We pray in the name of the Way,
　　the Truth, and the Life. Amen.

OPENING PRAYER

O God, our rock and our refuge,
　　our lives are in your hands.
In the midst of the Resurrection celebration,
　　and in the midst of everyday frustrations,
　　our lives are in your hands.
On the mountaintop and in the valley,
　　in the upper room and in the garden,
　　our lives are in your hands.
When our faith is strong, and when our faith is weak,
　　our lives are in your hands.
May we live each day in the glory of this certainty:
　　Our lives are in your hands.
Amen.

BENEDICTION

Go forth as God's chosen people.
Go forth, knowing that you travel with the Way,
    the Truth, and the Life.
Go forth in the Spirit to show God's glory to all the world.

BENEDICTION

Do you know where you are going?
We go the way of Jesus, who is the Way.
Do you know the One who goes with you?
We go with Jesus, who is God's Word made flesh.
Do you know the way to be saved?
We go to Jesus, who is our salvation.

MAY 1, 2005

Sixth Sunday of Easter
Judy Schultz

COLOR
White

SCRIPTURE READINGS
Acts 17:22-31; Psalm 66:8-20; 1 Peter 3:13-22; John 14:15-21

THEME IDEAS
As Pentecost approaches, the Gospel reading with Jesus' promise to send an Advocate is an appropriate focus for Sunday's worship. The idea that the Advocate is at work within our lives is hinted at in Paul's sermon before the Areopagus: encouraging the Athenians to search and grope for God, who is not far from us. This might also be the Sunday to encourage parishioners to discover God in personal narratives of "what he has done for me" (Psalm 66:16).

CALL TO WORSHIP (PSALM 66)
Praise God! Let the sound of God's praise be heard!
God has kept us among the living.
God has tested us and given us burdens to carry.
God has not let our feet slip.
Through fire and water,
God has brought us out to safety.

We cried aloud to God,
and God has heard our prayer.
Let us all worship the God
who blesses us with steadfast love.

CALL TO WORSHIP (ACTS 17)

Let us praise God, who has made the world
and everything in it.
Let us praise the Lord of heaven and earth.
From one ancestor, God has made all nations
to inhabit the earth.
The Lord has planted a yearning
within all people to search for God.
We are God's offspring, God's sons and daughters,
who are yearning for God.
The God whom we seek is near.
We have found God in the risen Christ.
Together let us worship God.
We will worship God together!

CONTEMPORARY GATHERING WORDS (ACTS 17)

People of God, come into God's holy presence!
God is known in the glorious resurrection of Jesus.
We saw God in the life of Jesus.
We saw God in the death of Jesus.
We see and know God in the resurrection of Jesus.
God is alive!
God is alive all around us.
God is alive within us!

PRAISE SENTENCES (ACTS 17, JOHN 14)

God has not left us orphaned. God abides with us.
Because Christ lives, we can live our lives!
Praise God for helping us live our lives!

PRAISE SENTENCES (PSALM 66)

Come and listen! Come and hear!
God has done great things for us!
God has been with us in tough times.
God has heard our prayers.
God has never left our side.
God's love is always with us.
Praise God for staying with us and loving us!

OPENING PRAYER (JOHN 14)

Holy and living God,
 on this bright day, you awaken us to new life.
Trees are in leaf, flowers are in bloom,
 and our hearts spring up with new hope.
Abide with us, Spirit of the living Christ,
 in this hour of worship and always. Amen.

OPENING PRAYER (ACTS 17)

Holy God,
 may our worship this day reveal you
 to all who have come here seeking you.
Through our singing and praying,
 and in our proclamation,
 make yourself known in love and power.
Be not far from each of us, we pray. Amen.

BENEDICTION (ACTS 17)

Go from this place, knowing you have found God.
 The God who is not far from us also goes with us.
In God you live and move and have your being.
 In God we will pray faithfully, act justly,
 and live joyfully.
Go in peace. Amen!

BENEDICTION (1 PETER 3)

Go from this place, eager to do good in God's name.
We will go forth eagerly.
Share hope with others.
Speak with gentleness and reverence.
**We will respect others' points of view,
yet be ready to share our faith.**
Be assured that you leave with God's blessing. Amen!
Amen!

MAY 8, 2005

Seventh Sunday of Easter/
Ascension Sunday/
Mother's Day/
Festival of the Christian Home
Paula McCutcheon

COLOR
White

ASCENSION READINGS
Acts 1:1-11; Psalm 47; Ephesians 1:15-23; Luke 24:44-53

SEVENTH SUNDAY OF EASTER READINGS
Acts 1:6-14; Psalm 68:1-10, 32-35; 1 Peter 4:12-14; 5:6-11;
John 17:1-11

THEME IDEAS
The New International Bible's discussion of Luke's version
of the Ascension is very helpful in focusing today's theme on
three significant actions of God toward ancient and modern-
day disciples: Christ saves, sends, and blesses. This empha-
sis is seen in all of the readings, whether they be those of the
Ascension or the Seventh Sunday of Easter. Even as Christ
ascends into heaven and leaves behind the earthly ministry
of Jesus, God continues that ministry through the very per-
sons who have been saved through Christ Jesus, sending

and blessing disciples so that others may find that same salvation, commissioning, and blessing for their lives.

CALL TO WORSHIP (PSALM 47, LUKE 24)

Clap your hands, all you peoples;
Shout to God with loud songs of joy!
Celebrate the risen Christ living and loving among us.
God's love washes over us.
Sing praises to God.
Sing praises to the risen Christ.

CALL TO WORSHIP (ACTS 1, LUKE 24)

The risen Christ lives among us,
calling us to be a blessing,
calling us to heal and transform the brokenness
and the violence of our world.
The risen Christ lives among us,
calling us to be a blessing,
calling us to seek out the marginalized
and those who need to experience God's love.
The risen Christ lives among us,
calling us to be a blessing,
calling us to be disciples to the world—
blessed, healed, and sent.

CONTEMPORARY GATHERING WORDS

Come into God's presence,
clapping and singing praises to the risen Christ.
Christ is alive and living with us!
Christ is blessing and saving us!
Christ is healing and sending us!
Let us worship together,
celebrating and praising the living Christ!

PRAISE SENTENCES (LUKE 24)

Praise God for our many blessings.
We are God's beloved children and God is with us.

The risen Christ saves us, heals us,
and brings us all into God's kingdom.
Praise God for our many blessings. Praise God!

PRAISE SENTENCES (PSALM 47)
Our God is an awesome God! God loves us.
God is always with us.
Even death cannot separate us from our God.
Sing praises and exaltations to our awesome God!

OPENING PRAYER
Ever present God,
we come to you longing to feel your presence.
As you reminded your disciples long ago,
help us to remember that we are not alone
on our journey of discipleship.
Guide us to see the risen Christ in our everyday lives,
and especially in the eyes of each other,
that we may bring healing and new life
into the broken and dead places of our world.
Amen.

OPENING PRAYER
Eternal God,
it is often difficult to feel that we are truly blessed,
that you have created us to be a blessing to the world.
We struggle to see your blessings in others,
especially in those who are different from ourselves.
Empower us to feel the joy and excitement
felt by Christ's disciples on that day of ascension,
that we will rise each day with a promise
to see the risen Christ in every part of our lives
and in everyone we meet. Amen.

PRAYER OF CONFESSION

Living Christ,
  why are we so afraid to see you,
  to feel you,
  to hear you,
  and to listen to you?
Is it because when we turn to you,
  you call us to a ministry of salvation and healing?
Is it because when we are called,
  we must choose to follow you
    and share our God-given blessings with others?
Are we afraid to be your instruments
  of healing and wholeness?
Risen Christ,
  forgive our hardness of heart.
Help us to open ourselves completely to you,
  that we might continue the incredible mission
    and ministry you began through your disciples
      on that Ascension Day. Amen.

BENEDICTION

Blessed! Saved! Healed and Whole!
We are sent to bring blessing,
  healing, and love into our world.

BENEDICTION

The risen Christ is with us.
Let us give thanks for God's eternal presence with us.
Let us go forth, sharing the good news
  of God's blessing and healing.

MAY 15, 2005

Pentecost Sunday
Mary J. Scifres

COLOR
Red

SCRIPTURE READINGS
Acts 2:1-21; Psalm 104:24-34, 35*b*; 1 Corinthians 12:3*b*-13; John 7:37-39

THEME IDEAS
Pentecost Sunday evokes images of doves and bright flames, red garments and festive decorations. These images express our desire to celebrate and honor the Holy Spirit's presence in our lives and in our worship. When we allow the grace and indwelling of the Spirit to flow through our worship, the transforming power of the Holy Spirit comes alive within our congregations. Pentecost Sunday is a time to rekindle our elders' dreams and ideals for God's realm on earth and to encourage our youth's visions and hopes for Christ's presence in our world.

CALL TO WORSHIP (ACTS 2)
Pour out your Holy Spirit,
  that we might be your sons and daughters.
Pour out your Holy Spirit,
  that we might prophesy in your holy name.
Pour out your Holy Spirit,

that we might see visions of justice and mercy.
Pour out your Holy Spirit,
that we might dream dreams of hope and peace.
Pour out your Holy Spirit,
that we might be your daughters and sons.

CALL TO WORSHIP (JOHN 7)

Come, all who are thirsty.
Christ invites us to the fountain of life.
Drink of the living water.
We yearn to quench our thirst.
Believe, and be filled by the fullness of God.
The love of Christ will overflow in our lives.
Let the river of justice flow over and through us.
We pray to be fountains of living water.
Pray, and trust that our prayers will be answered.
The Spirit will guide us forward.

CONTEMPORARY GATHERING WORDS (ACTS 2)

Come let us call upon the Lord!
I will call upon the Lord!
We await the coming of Christ.
I will call upon the Lord!
We trust in the promises of God.
I will call upon the Lord!
We feel the presence of God's Spirit.
I will call upon the Lord!
Come let us call upon the Lord!

PRAISE SENTENCES (PSALM 104)

Bless the LORD, O my soul! Praise the LORD!
Bless the LORD, O my soul! Praise the LORD!
Rejoice in the LORD always! Again, we say rejoice!
Rejoice! Rejoice!

OPENING PRAYER (ACTS 2)

Come upon us, Holy Spirit.
Rush through this place of worship.

Gather us into your holy presence.
Grant us your word,
    that all that we say and all that we do
        may proclaim the power and might
            of your glorious light. Amen.

PRAYER OF THANKSGIVING (PSALM 104)

We look to you for so many things, gracious God,
    and in due season, you give us everything we need—
        food from the earth, water from the skies,
        and companionship for your human creation.
Just as we gather up these many gifts during our lives,
    we now gather up these gifts to give back to you.
Send these gifts forth with your Spirit.
Create with these gifts your kingdom here on earth.
Bless our giving that we might give fully and freely
In your loving name, we offer thanks and praise.
Amen.

CLOSING PRAYER (ACTS 2)

As we leave this place,
    send us forth with your Spirit of truth and grace.
Let your visions and dreams inspire our ministry,
    that we might inspire the world.
Amen and amen.

RESPONSIVE READING OR BENEDICTION (1 CORINTHIANS 12)

Let us be the body of Christ.
    We are one body, consisting of many members.
Let us be the ministers of Christ.
    We are one in ministry, called to be the Church.
Let us be the gifts of God.
    We are all gifted, with diversity and creativity.
Let us be the blessings of God.
    We are all blessed, inspired by the Holy Spirit.

BENEDICTION (PENTECOST)
Go forth, filled with the Spirit of God.
Let the Spirit flow through you
   that our world may be inspired
   with the hope of Christ Jesus.
Go in peace. Amen.

MAY 22, 2005

Trinity Sunday
Robert Blezard

COLOR
White

SCRIPTURE READINGS
Genesis 1:1–2:4*a*; Psalm 8; 2 Corinthians 13:11-13; Matthew 28:16-20

THEME IDEAS
Human beings enjoy a special relationship with God and to the rest of the created order. Unlike all other elements of creation, human beings are made in God's image and are bestowed with authority and stewardship over the earth. Jesus gives his followers an additional responsibility: to make disciples of all nations; and the church gives us another: to baptize new Christians "in the name of the Father and of the Son and of the Holy Spirit." On Trinity Sunday, we remember our responsibilities, delight in the trust that God has given us, and pray for guidance to complete our tasks with faithfulness.

CALL TO WORSHIP (GENESIS 1)
Let us remember what our God has done!
God created the world out of a formless void.
Let us remember what our God has done!
God made every animal and plant, bird and fish.

Let us remember what our God has done!
God created people in the image of God.
Let us remember what our God has done!
God has made us caretakers of the earth.
Let us complete our task in faithfulness.

CALL TO WORSHIP (PSALM 8)

Who are we, O God, that you draw near when we call?
Your faithful people call your name.
Who are we, O God, that you care for us?
Your faithful people call your name.
Who are we, O God, that you crown us with honor?
Your faithful people call your name.
Who are we, O God, that you make us stewards
of the earth?
Your faithful people call your name.
Who are we, O God, to deserve your faith and trust?
Your faithful people call your name.

CONTEMPORARY GATHERING WORDS (PSALM 8)

God is with us, right here and now.
We open our lives to our creator.
God cares for us and gives us glory.
We open our hearts to our creator.
God appoints us keepers of the earth.
We dedicate ourselves to our creator.

PRAISE SENTENCES (GENESIS 1)

Blessed are you, O God, creator of all that is.
Blessed are you, O God, creator of all that will be.
Blessed are you, O God, who made us in your image.
Praised be your name! Amen.

PRAISE SENTENCES (PSALM 8)

How majestic is your name in all the earth!
You have set your glory above the heavens.

O God, creative Spirit, all things have their beginning
  and ending in you. We hold your name on high.
Glory and honor to you! Amen.

OPENING PRAYER (GENESIS 1)
Eternal God,
    your Spirit moved on the waters—
      and there was light,
      your first creation.
  your Spirit moved on the water of our baptism—
      and again, there was light in our souls and hearts.
  Let your holy light shine on us today,
    as we remember your creation
      and our special part in it. Amen.

OPENING PRAYER (PSALM 8)
From the time you fashioned the heavens and the earth
    from a formless void, O God,
    your creative energy has done marvelous works,
    all around us.
May your creative Spirit
    be at work in our hearts and minds today
    as we worship you and, always,
    as we strive to live in obedience to your will. Amen.

PRAYER OF CONFESSION (GENESIS 1)
Holy and merciful God, in perfection you created the
earth, fixed the course of the sun and seasons, and popu-
lated the earth with plants, fish, birds, and animals to live
in an intricate, balanced web of life. You created us in
your image and gave us the responsibility to care for the
world. We confess that we have failed to live up to our
responsibilities. Our lust for comfort and money has polluted the water with industrial wastes, sewage, fertilizer,
and pesticide runoff. We choke the air with gases that not
only poison both plants and animals but also change the

earth's climate, at great peril. We have cut too many trees to sell lumber or build houses. We have drained too many fertile marshes and wetlands to create usable land. We have destroyed too many wildlife habitats in the name of progress. For these sins of commission and omission, we are heartily sorry. We pray your forgiveness and beg that you would create a right heart and mind within us, that we may consume according to our need instead of our want and that we may begin to heal your creation from human injury. Amen.

PRAYER OF CONFESSION (GENESIS 1, MATTHEW 28)
Holy and eternal God,
>you created us in your image
>>and gave us special responsibilities toward creation
>>and our fellow human beings.

You set us as caretakers for the earth
>and all its plants and animals.

You anointed us as disciples
>and told us to make fellow disciples the world over.

Dear God, as we look at our polluted earth,
>where we consume resources at an unsustainable rate,
>we know that we have failed to be good stewards.

In many ways,
>we have failed to live as disciples ourselves,
>to say nothing of making disciples of all nations.

We beg your mercy for our sins
>and await with expectancy
>>the renewal of our minds and hearts,
>>that we may devote the rest of our days
>>to protecting the earth and making disciples
>>of all nations in accordance to your will. Amen.

BENEDICTION (GENESIS 1, PSALM 8)
May God's creative Spirit be with us in our hearts
>and minds as we leave this place to return home.

May God's creative Spirit help us to see with new wonder
the splendor of your creation all around us
and inspire us to preserve and protect it.

BENEDICTION (GENESIS 1, PSALM 8)
God has accomplished marvelous things!
We are part of creation's fulfillment.
Let us go in new appreciation
for the works of God's hands.
We are part of creation's fulfillment.
Let us work to restore the earth's perfect balance
and beauty.
We are part of creation's fulfillment.
Let us live as faithful disciples,
telling all what God has done.
We are part of creation's fulfillment.
And remember that Jesus is always with us,
to the end of the age.
We are part of creation's fulfillment.

MAY 29, 2005

Second Sunday After Pentecost
Robert Blezard

COLOR
    Green

SCRIPTURE READINGS
    Genesis 6:9-22; 7:24; 8:14-19; Psalm 46; Romans 1:16-17;
    3:22b-28 (29-31); Matthew 7:21-29

THEME IDEAS
    Human sinfulness has corrupted God's perfect creation
    from the earliest, but God is eager to save those who turn
    their hearts and souls to God. Noah found favor with God,
    and so when God caused a flood to cleanse the earth of its
    corruption, Noah and his family were not only spared but
    also given a special role in a second creation. The Psalter and
    Gospel readings reinforce this theme. Disasters and calami-
    ties befall every life, imperil many souls, but those who trust
    in God make it through with divine assistance and salvation.
    The epistle and Gospel readings make it clear that the saving
    work of God is through Jesus Christ, given in God's grace to
    those who, like Noah, believe and do God's will.

CALL TO WORSHIP (PSALM 46, MATTHEW 7)
    Winds blow, storms rage.
        God is our refuge.
    Floods rise, waves batter.

God is our refuge.
Wars ravage, violence threatens.
God is our refuge.
Corruption rules, greed reigns.
God is our refuge.
We cry to God; God hears us.
God is our refuge.
We are safe; we are warm.
Thanks be to God.

CALL TO WORSHIP (ROMANS 1)

Come, let us remember the graciousness of God.
The gospel is the power of God for salvation!
Let us remember the graciousness of God.
**We are redeemed through the sacrifice
of Christ Jesus.**
Let us remember the graciousness of God.
We rejoice in God's generous gift of life.
Let us remember the graciousness of God.

CONTEMPORARY GATHERING WORDS (MATTHEW 7)

Outside, the storms of life batter us.
We seek refuge here with God.
The winds howl and rattle the windows.
God makes us secure and safe.
Floods rise and whisk away many.
God is our rock, our sure foundation.
Let us worship God, our strength.

CONTEMPORARY GATHERING WORDS (GENESIS 6)

Let's face it, life is hard.
But God is always our friend.
Violence and greed surround us.
But God is always our friend.
Newspapers are full of bad news.

But God is always our friend.
We call out to God, who seeks to save us.
God is always our friend.

PRAISE SENTENCES (PSALM 46)
Like a river, O God, you flow through our lives.
Your streams satisfy our deepest thirsts.
Your cascades delight and refresh us.
Where your waters flow there is peace,
there is safety, there is justice!

PRAISE SENTENCES (ROMANS 1)
Your redeeming grace, O God, is boundless!
We are saved through the sacrifice of your son, Jesus.
A gift to your people, bestowed out of love!
Your mercy knows no depth.

PRAISE SENTENCES (PSALM 46)
There is no power greater than our God.
At God's command, tumult is silenced, warring ceases.
God is exalted throughout all the earth.

OPENING PRAYER (GENESIS 6)
God of mercy and redemption,
    be with us today.
As we gather in this place,
    safe from the storms of life that rage outside,
    be our strength and our refuge.
We open our hearts and minds to you;
    fill them with your joy and your love,
    your peace and your reassurance. Amen.

OPENING PRAYER (MATTHEW 7)
Lord, Lord,
    we call to you in our desire to know you
        and to make your ways our own.
Teach us, take us, transform us,
that we may serve you with our whole selves

and do the will of our God in heaven.
Lord, Lord,
   be with us now. Amen.

PRAYER OF CONFESSION (ROMANS 1, MATTHEW 7)

God has created the world perfect and whole,
but human sin has corrupted it
and filled it with violence.
   We are sinful and fall short of the glory of God.
We call you, "Lord, Lord," with our lips,
but our hearts are lustful and impure.
   We are sinful and fall short of the glory of God.
We consume far too much
without giving thought to millions who starve.
   We are sinful and fall short of the glory of God.
Our destructive wars take innocent lives
and cause people to live in fear.
   We are sinful and fall short of the glory of God.
But in faith, we throw ourselves on your mercy, Lord,
and pray for your forgiveness and guidance.
   We are sinful and fall short of the glory of God.
You have redeemed your people
through the sacrifice of your son, Jesus Christ.
   We are sinful and fall short of the glory of God.
As your faithful, forgiven people,
we hunger for your guidance and love,
that we might know and do your will.
   Thanks be to God.

BENEDICTION

Go in peace amid life's storms.
   God is our safe harbor.
Go in peace amid life's floods.
   God is our high ground.
Go in peace in a violent world.
   God is our strength and protection.
Go in God's peace.
   Amen.

JUNE 5, 2005

Third Sunday After Pentecost
Mary J. Scifres

COLOR
Green

SCRIPTURE READINGS
Genesis 12:1-9; Psalm 33:1-12; Romans 4:13-25; Matthew 9:9-13, 18-26

THEME IDEAS
In today's readings, faith and grace arise as primary foci. The faith of Abraham is exhibited in the Genesis reading and exalted in Paul's letter to the Romans. In Matthew's Gospel, the faith of the hemorrhaging woman and the desperate father are juxtaposed against the judgmental legalism of the Pharisees. In all of these readings, the grace of God makes human faith possible, allowing God's miraculous intervention into human history. What a wonderful circle of life. We are invited to enter into this faith, allowing God to then enter into the human story, which leads to further faith on humanity's part! Truly, this is a never-ending cycle we can all celebrate.

CALL TO WORSHIP (PSALM 33)
Rejoice in the LORD, righteous children of God!
We come with joyful praise,
worshiping the One who makes us righteous!

Sing a glad song to God, loving followers of Christ!
We come with strings and voices of joy,
singing to the One who gives us love!
Shout aloud in hope, children of the Spirit!
We come with awe and admiration,
rejoicing in the One who is among us now!

CALL TO WORSHIP (MATTHEW 9)

Come into the presence of God!
All are welcome here!
Come, sinners and saints alike!
We are the children of God.
Christ is with us now.
God's love will heal our wounds.
Christ has called us here.
We rejoice in God's gracious love.

CONTEMPORARY GATHERING WORDS (PSALM 33)

Come into the Lord's presence.
Sing a new song to God!
We sing with praise and joy!
Rejoice in the Lord of love.
Sing a new song to God!
We sing with praise and joy!
Seek justice and righteousness.
Sing a new song to God!
We sing with praise and joy!
Come together in worship.
Sing a new song to God!
We sing with praise and joy!

PRAISE SENTENCES (PSALM 33)

Rejoice in the Lord!
Sing a new song!
Rejoice in the Lord!
Sing God's glorious praise!

OPENING PRAYER (PSALM 33)

God of justice and righteousness,
    bring your Word into our lives.
Rain down your Spirit upon us,
    creating steadfast hearts of love and mercy within us.
Breathe new life into our tired souls,
    inspiring us to live as your faithful followers.
Counsel our troubled minds,
    guiding us on paths of justice and righteousness.
In faith and hope, we pray. Amen.

OPENING PRAYER (ROMANS 4)

Faithful and loving God,
    give us a faith that removes all doubt.
Help us to live as people
    who trust in you at all times
    and in all places.
We come to you now,
    hoping against hope,
    looking for your presence in our world.
We enter this time of worship,
    believing in your promise,
    glorifying and praising your name.
Where there is doubt or distrust,
    give us a renewed faith.
Where there is fear or insecurity,
    give us newfound courage.
Where there is fatigue or weakness,
    give us amazing strength.
Where there is darkness or confusion,
    give us the light of your wisdom.
Where there is sorrow or loss,
    give us comforting peace.
In all of these things,

help us to know that your promises are true
    and your loving presence is steadfast.
In Christ's name we pray. Amen.

PRAYER OF CONFESSION (MATTHEW 9)
Merciful God,
    we confess that we have not always been as merciful
        as you call us to be.
For those times when we have judged others,
    forgive us, gracious God.
For those times when we have doubted your mercy,
    grant mercy in our lives.
When we waver in our grace and kindness,
    heal us and make us whole,
    that our mercy and forgiveness
        might be steadfast and true.
In all that we say and all that we do,
    help us to live as your children,
    forgiven and reconciled
        by the grace of Christ Jesus. Amen.

WORDS OF ASSURANCE (MATTHEW 9)
Believe in Christ's grace, your faith has made you well.
In trusting God's grace, we are all forgiven.
In Christ, we are all made whole!

CLOSING PRAYER (GENESIS 12)
God of Abraham and Sarah,
    bless us that we might be a blessing to others.
Send us forth into your world,
    showing us the way you would have us go.
Help us to bless with your love and grace
    all whom we meet.
In your name, we pray. Amen.

BENEDICTION (ROMANS 4, MATTHEW 9)
And now, dear friends, go forth with unwavering faith.
Trust that we have been made righteous

through the grace and love of Christ Jesus.
With that trust, go into the world,
   sharing our faith and showing others
that our faith has made us well! Go in peace!

BENEDICTION (GENESIS 12)

Go from this place
   into the places that God will show you.
Christ has made us God's children and has blessed us,
   making our name great.
In the name of Christ, go forth as a blessing to others!

JUNE 12, 2005

Fourth Sunday After Pentecost
Christine S. Boardman

COLOR
Green

SCRIPTURE READINGS
Genesis 18:1-15 (21:1-7); Psalm 116:1-2, 12-19; Romans 5:1-8; Matthew 9:35–10:8 (9-23)

THEME IDEAS
When we least expect it, God arrives in the form of a stranger. How are we to respond? What are we willing to share with the least, the lost, and the lonely? It seems safer to take care of ourselves and not to venture too far from security. Surely God jests with us when we are called to give of ourselves without counting the cost. We might say we are too old, too weak, or too uncertain. When Christ came, God's realm came closer. How would we change our priorities to reflect God's realm? Today the church and the disciples of Jesus have a high calling: to recognize how God would have us respond and live with faith as bearers of the good news. How can we live with God's possibility, potential, and promise?

CALL TO WORSHIP (ROMANS 5)
Come, friends in Christ,
let us worship at the throne of God.

We are here to receive God's grace.
Come, friends in Christ,
let us worship at the foot of the cross.
**We are here to grow stronger in our faith
in Christ Jesus.**
Come, friends in Christ,
let us worship with hopeful hearts.
We will worship in spirit and in truth.

CALL TO WORSHIP (MATTHEW 9)

Jesus has called us to proclaim the good news
of God's redeeming love.
**We come to worship as people who have heard
and responded to God's call in Jesus Christ.**
Jesus has called us to heal the nations
and bring hope to all we meet.
**We come from all races and cultures
to be Christ's disciples.**
Jesus has called us to demonstrate compassion
and commitment.
**We come as disciples to worship
and gain strength for our journey.
Let us worship God together. Alleluia!**

CONTEMPORARY GATHERING WORDS (PSALM 116)

Come into God's presence.
We call upon God.
Lift your voices to God.
We call upon God.
Offer thanksgiving to the Lord of Life.
We call upon God.
Let us gather to worship God.

PRAISE SENTENCES (GENESIS 18)

We laugh when God surprises us with possibility.
We laugh and love and lift our voices to a great God.

We love when God surprises us with new birth.
We laugh and love and lift our voices to a great God.

OPENING PRAYER

O God, we come into your gracious presence
preoccupied with our cares,
afraid to face our emptiness.
Disclose your wisdom
in the reading of your Holy Word,
and in the proclamation of your gospel.
May our labors be pleasing to you,
and may we be inspired to proclaim the good news
of Jesus our Sovereign. Amen.

OFFERTORY PRAYER

Dear God of possibility, potential, and promise,
we offer our lives as laborers in your field.
We offer you gifts of financial resources
from the blessings we have received from you.
May our offerings be a source of healing and wholeness
to others as well as to ourselves.
Visit us as stranger and as Savior
that in our living we may laugh, love,
and proclaim the good news of Christ's coming.
In the name of our Shepherd and our Sovereign, we pray.
Amen.

BENEDICTION

Go now with compassion.
Go now in peace.
God's realm has come and we bear good news.
May the healing presence of our Savior
guide and direct you to proclaim the good news.

BENEDICTION

Go now into the world to lend yourselves
to God's work of love.

We go with the blessing of God who creates us.
Go now into the world to see with compassionate eyes.
We go with the blessing of God who redeems us.
Go now into the world to offer kindness and courage
to others.
We go with the blessing of God who sustains us.
And let God's people say amen.
Amen.

JUNE 19, 2005

Fifth Sunday After Pentecost/ Father's Day

Robert Blezard

COLOR

Green

SCRIPTURE READINGS

Genesis 21:8-21; Psalm 86:1-10, 16-17; Romans 6:1*b*-11; Matthew 10:24-39

THEME IDEAS

God's love for us is infinite, and the bond between us and our heavenly parent is stronger than family ties in our earthly lives. This theme is introduced with Hagar and Ishmael, expelled from the family nest and sent off to the desert with only a skin of water and some bread. (Banished by none other than Abraham himself!) But God has plans for Hagar, and especially for Ishmael, and saves them from thirst and hunger, offering them a new beginning. The Psalter reinforces the idea of God's aid in our time of need. In Romans, Paul emphasizes new life under the reign of God, when the old self—and by extension its relationships—is left for dead. In the Gospel reading, Jesus teaches about God's great love for every individual and cautions that our love for God should trump earthly allegiances.

CALL TO WORSHIP (PSALM 86)

We gather together as family.
God is our heavenly parent.
We gather united as brothers and sisters.
God is our heavenly parent.
We gather to praise and worship in gladness.
God is our heavenly parent.
We gather to sing hymns of thanksgiving.
God is our heavenly parent.
We gather to raise up prayers and petitions.
God is our heavenly parent.
And we gather to listen to God's loving voice.
Praise God, our heavenly parent.

CALL TO WORSHIP (ROMANS 6, MATTHEW 10)

Today we recall what God has done:
Proclaim it from the housetops.
God's saving work in Jesus Christ,
Proclaim it from the housetops.
Resurrecting us into new life,
Proclaim it from the housetops.
Releasing us from the power of sin and death,
Proclaim it from the housetops.
Alive to God forevermore.
We tell it in the light.

CONTEMPORARY GATHERING WORDS (MATTHEW 10)

From many paths and many pasts,
we come together as family,
with Christ as our brother,
and God as our father and mother.
We are united as family by God's boundless,
endless love,
with Christ as our brother,
and God as our father and mother.

Even the hairs on our head are counted.
In God, we are known,
by Christ our brother,
and God our father and mother.
We speak God's truth and proclaim it from the housetops,
that Christ is our brother,
and God is our father and mother.
In our heavenly family, we are loved and feel no fear.
Thanks to God above.

Praise Sentences (Psalm 86)
There is none like you, O God, our father and mother.
You are our help and comfort in times of trouble.
You lift up the lowly and heed the cries of the downtrodden.
We will glorify your name forever.

Praise Sentences (Matthew 10)
Can any words describe God's love for you,
a love that is vaster than space
and deeper than midnight?
Among billions of people, God calls you by name,
peers into your heart,
and counts the hair on your head.
God weeps with your sorrows and delights in your joys.
God calls you as a son or a daughter, as family.
You share in the celebration of life's mysteries.
Can any words describe God's love for you,
a love that is vaster than space
and deeper than midnight?

Opening Prayer (Psalm 86)
O God,
your children call to you,
for all the things you do.
Hold us close to thee, bounce us on your knee,
listen to our woes, wipe our runny nose,

rock us off to sleep, give us comfort when we weep,
keep us safe from harm, keep us safe and warm.
Your children you adore,
now and forevermore. Amen.

OPENING PRAYER (MATTHEW 10)

God of love,
you peer into each soul and heart
and cherish us just the same.
Be with us now as we come into your presence
with reverence and humility,
with joy and expectation.
Help us to live more fully
with the realization of your endless love for us.
Teach us to live and love as a family.
Guide us to be good children,
as you are our perfect parent. Amen.

OPENING PRAYER (PSALM 86)

Be with us, O God,
and be gracious with your needy servants.
To you we bring the cares of our lives,
the deepest yearnings of our souls.
Strengthen us, we pray,
by the healing balm of your love
and the steadfast guidance of your teachings.
We lift up our hands
and open our hearts
to embrace your transforming love. Amen.

PRAYER OF CONFESSION (MATTHEW 10)

We confess that we have not lived as your children.
Have mercy on us.
Forgetting your endless love for us,
we have been paralyzed by fear.
Have mercy on us.

We have failed to reveal your light,
failed to proclaim your truth from the housetops.
>**Have mercy on us.**
We have not acknowledged Jesus Christ before others.
>**Have mercy on us.**
We have loved others more than we love you, O God.
>**Have mercy on us.**
Help us hold firm to your promise to love and cherish us.
>**Have mercy on us.**
Never give up on your children.
>**Have mercy on us.**
Forgive us, lead us and teach us.
>**We are yours forever. Amen.**

BENEDICTION

May the love of God our father,
the comfort of God our mother,
and the joy of Jesus our brother,
be with you now and always.
>**Amen.**

BENEDICTION (MATTHEW 10)

Be fearless!
>**We are God's family.**
Speak the truth!
>**We are God's family.**
Proclaim Christ!
>**We are God's family.**
Go in peace!
>**We are God's family.**
>**Thanks be to God.**

JUNE 26, 2005

Sixth Sunday After Pentecost
B. J. Beu

COLOR
Green

SCRIPTURE READINGS
Genesis 22:1-14; Psalm 13; Romans 6:12-23; Matthew 10:40-42

THEME IDEAS
Life is full of pain and trials. We face trials of faith, as we seek God's comfort and protection (Psalm 13). We endure trials of conflicting loyalties, as we struggle to follow God while living with personal integrity (Genesis 22). We succumb to trials of earthly passions and sinful temptations, even as we aspire to be made holy in our walk with Christ (Romans 6). And we meet trials of social status, as we struggle with the lack of recognition for leading godly lives (Matthew 10). In the midst of our pain and fears of abandonment, God is there to rescue us and lead us safely home.

CALL TO WORSHIP (PSALM 13)
You seem far away, O Lord.
Yet we trust in your goodness and mercy.
Do not hide your face from us forever, O God.
We put our trust in your steadfast love.
How long shall our souls bear this pain, O Lord?

Our hearts will rejoice in your salvation.
How long shall our enemies exalt over us, O God?
We will sing to the Lord, who is our hope.

CALL TO WORSHIP (GENESIS 22)

Our faith is sorely tested.
God calls for a sacrifice.
How can we put another to the knife?
Faith demands a choice.
Wait! Look, a ram in the thicket.
God has provided the offering.
The test of faith is over.
Deliverance is at hand.

CONTEMPORARY GATHERING WORDS (MATTHEW 10)

In Christ Jesus you are welcome here.
In Christ Jesus we are welcome.
Welcome the One who sent Christ to save us.
We welcome God into our midst.
Welcome prophets and little children in Christ's name.
We welcome the people of God.

PRAISE SENTENCES

Rejoice in God! Sing to the Lord!
God has blessed us! The Lord has lifted us up!
Rejoice in God! Sing to the Lord!

OPENING PRAYER (MATTHEW 10)

Welcoming God,
We come to you as we are,
seeking approval,
seeking forgiveness,
seeking to find our way home.
Help us welcome others,
as we would like to be welcomed.

Teach us to value the rewards that come
   from a life of servanthood.
Help us embrace the cost of discipleship,
   that we may be welcomed into your eternal home.
   Amen.

OPENING PRAYER (GENESIS 22)
Merciful God,
   we go through life feeling tested.
Whenever anything goes wrong,
   we wonder,
      what have I done to deserve this?
Help us remember that you seek our salvation,
   not our pain.
Remind us that your ways lead to life,
   not death.
Teach us again that you are holy and just,
   abiding in steadfast love,
   that we might rise above our doubts
      and embrace your mercy. Amen.

PRAYER OF CONFESSION
Eternal God,
   it is easier to ask, "How long will we suffer?"
      than to remember that our suffering is lessened
         when we place our faith in you.
It is easier to question why our enemies flourish,
   than to remember that they are your children too.
Forgive our self-centered ways, O God,
   and help us celebrate the salvation we find in you,
   through Jesus Christ our Lord. Amen.

ASSURANCE OF PARDON (ROMANS 6)
Once we were slaves to sin,
   but now we are free to be a righteous people.
God is here, extending the hand of love to all
   who seek the source of true life.

BENEDICTION

Go forth as God's people, transformed and made whole.
Go forth to live lives worthy of the gospel,
    lives worthy of our calling in Christ Jesus.

BENEDICTION (GENESIS 22)

The God who set Isaac free is here to set our hearts free.
    We have been released from bondage
    and go forth with hearts full of joy.
The God who has set our hearts free is sending us forth
to free a world enslaved by worry and doubt.
    We go forth, to loose the cords of the bound,
    and heal the wounds of the afflicted.
Go with God.

JULY 3, 2005

Seventh Sunday After Pentecost
Kristi Hanson Kreamer

COLOR

Green

SCRIPTURE READINGS

Genesis 24:34-38, 42-49, 58-67; Psalm 45:10-17; Romans 7:15-25a; Matthew 11:16-19, 25-30

THEME IDEAS

This Sunday serves as a warning to the proud and an offer of comfort to the meek. The Genesis reading and the Psalm both tell of brides whose humble obedience to God's purpose is richly rewarded. In the Gospel lesson, the wisdom of God is hidden from the spiritually arrogant and is revealed instead to those with childlike faith. Jesus promises relief to all who have grown weary and are burdened with religious striving. Paul's words to the Romans echo this reassurance to those despairing under fruitless moral effort. In our weakness before sin, it is not our achievements but Christ's rescue that is our hope.

CALL TO WORSHIP (MATTHEW 11, ROMANS 7)

Let those who seek to please God with their goodness hear the good news.
Christ will be our goodness!
Let those who are burdened with guilt for their failures hear the good news.

144

Christ will accomplish all for us
and quiet our hearts!
Take up the discipline of grace.
We will embrace the disciplines
that empowers us to live as God intends!
Learn the ways of Christ.
The Lord will not condemn us
but will fill our souls with peace!

CALL TO WORSHIP (MATTHEW 11)
Let us enter God's presence with joy.
For our Lord is gentle and humble in heart!
Let God's Word relieve you of pride.
For our Lord is gentle and humble in heart!
Give your failings and burdens to God.
For our Lord is gentle and humble in heart!
Live with joy.
Christ's yoke is easy. God's burden is light!

CONTEMPORARY GATHERING WORDS (GENESIS 24, PSALM 45)
People of God, we are the church, the bride of Christ.
Today we are invited by God's Word
to leave behind our old loyalties
and to bow our wills before our bridegroom in humility.
God promises us many blessings
when we stop insisting on doing things our own way.
God offers us many blessings
when we embrace the joy of discipleship.
Let it be so with us today and always.

CONTEMPORARY GATHERING WORDS (MATTHEW 11)
Jesus says, "Come to me, all you that are weary
and are carrying heavy burdens, and I will give you
rest." Dear friends, Christ is here offering us rest.

We cast our cares upon God.
Take Christ's love and wear it well,
for this garment is easy and light.
We cast our cares upon God.
Come into this place of love,
where we worship a gentle God.
We cast our cares upon God.

PRAISE SENTENCES (PSALM 45)

Grace is with us now. Glory to God on high!
Grace is with us now. Glory to God on high!
(Mary Scifres)

CALL TO WORSHIP OR PRAYER OF CONFESSION (ROMANS 7)

We enter God's presence through the gift of grace.
Thanks be to God through Jesus Christ!
Even when our actions do not match our intentions,
we are welcome in the house of God.
Thanks be to God through Jesus Christ!
Even when we fall away from God,
we are forgiven and made whole in God's sight.
Thanks be to God through Jesus Christ!
Even when we are discouraged by our failings,
we are forgiven and empowered to live a new life.
Thanks be to God through Jesus Christ!

OPENING PRAYER

God of wisdom and mercy,
In your kingdom, the lowly are made great
as they wait upon you and receive your grace.
Open our hearts to this kingdom today.
Renew in us a childlike faith,
as we hear your word and sing your praises,
that we might go from this place
proclaiming the good news of the gospel.
Amen.

UNISON PRAYER

Gracious Lord,
   help us trust your goodness and gentle humility,
   that we might bring our failings before you.
In our weakness, grant us the certainty
   that we are made strong by relying on Christ,
   who is our truth and our salvation. Amen.

CALL TO PRAYER

Let us acknowledge to ourselves and to God
the sin in our lives that has burdened and wounded us.

PRAYER OF CONFESSION (MATTHEW 11)

Loving Savior,
   we confess that we want to feel powerful
      and in control of our lives and destinies.
We too often become entangled in our own schemes
   to earn your favor and prove our worthiness.
Forgive our proud religious sophistication.
Forgive us for judging others
   when they fail to measure up to our scrutiny.
Give us humble hearts,
   that we might embrace your mercy for ourselves
      and reflect it to others. Amen.

WORDS OF ASSURANCE (MATTHEW 11)

Children of God, in humility and gentleness,
   Christ came to forgive you and renew your life.
You have been rescued from the power of sin
   by the Lord Jesus Christ.
Let your hearts be content and your witness made bold
   as you walk in the freedom of God's grace.

BENEDICTION (MATTHEW 11)

Rejoice and take God's word of encouragement
   with you as you go forth!

Let go of pride.
Lean on God's grace.
Learn from Christ, our teacher.
Live for your neighbor!

BENEDICTION (GENESIS 24)
May we leave this place renewed and empowered,
    following God's call to be servants in Christ's name.
May we have faith and courage like Rebekah,
    leaving behind our old lives to follow the will of God!

JULY 10, 2005

Eighth Sunday After Pentecost

Mary J. Scifres

COLOR
Green

SCRIPTURE READINGS
Genesis 25:19-34; Psalm 119:105-112; Romans 8:1-11; Matthew 13:1-9, 18-23

THEME IDEAS
Each of today's scriptures stands alone in message and theme, woven together loosely by a focus on the Word of God. From Genesis, we continue the epic stories of our faith, hearing of the birth of Jacob and Esau and the roots of conflict that would plague their lives. Psalm 119 focuses on the law as a life-giving blessing. Romans, on the other hand, promises that God's law has now been transformed into God's grace through Christ Jesus. Finally, Matthew's message emphasizes that the word is transformed only when planted and nurtured in the fertile soil of faithful followers.

CALL TO WORSHIP (PSALM 119, MATTHEW 13)
In love and tenderness, God's Word has been planted in our hearts.
May the Word of God light our ways
as we worship together.
In praise and joy, we come to hear and study God's Word.

May the Word of God light our ways
as we worship together.
In faith and hope, we listen for Christ's call
in God's Word.
We rejoice, knowing that the Word of God
will light our ways as we worship together!

CALL TO WORSHIP (ROMANS 8)

We have been invited into the presence of God.
As we enter, we set our minds
on the things of the Spirit.
Let this Spirit be the Spirit of life and peace.
For this Spirit is the Spirit of God.
We live in this Spirit,
for this Spirit of God dwells within us.
We live in this Spirit,
for this is the Christ living within us.
We live in this Spirit,
for this Spirit is the Holy One sustaining us.
We live in this Spirit
both now and forevermore.

CONTEMPORARY GATHERING WORDS (PSALM 119)

Thy word is a lamp unto my feet,
and a light unto my path.
God's Word is our light!
Thy word is a lamp unto my feet,
and a light unto my path.
God's Word is our light!

PRAISE SENTENCES (PSALM 119, MATTHEW 13)

Praise God for the Word.
Praise God for the Holy Word!
Praise God for love.
Praise God for everlasting love!

OPENING PRAYER (MATTHEW 13)

God of wisdom,
    let your word fall upon us this day.
Let your law of love embed itself in our hearts.
Let your grace and mercy take root in our lives.
Open our hearts to your nurture,
    that we may grow in faith.
Open our lives to your guidance,
    that we may grow in service.
Send your Holy Spirit upon us,
    that we may become true disciples of Jesus Christ.
Amen.

OPENING PRAYER (PSALM 119)

Gracious God,
    open our hearts to your word this day.
Light our paths
    with the brightness of your love and wisdom.
Guide us as we seek to walk in your ways
    and grow in your truth.
Accept our offerings of praise,
    that our songs and our words may be transformed
        into your songs and your words.
In Christ's name, we pray. Amen.

PRAYER (GENESIS 25, MATTHEW 13)

Loving God,
    help us to grow as we face the struggles of this life.
When we are in conflict,
    help us to learn the true meaning of forgiveness.
When we are in turmoil,
    grant us your peace that passes all understanding.
When our roots are shallow or bitter,
    replant us in fertile soil of loving faith.
When we wrestle with doubts,
    give us faith seeking understanding.

When the woes of this world threaten us,
    help us lean on your nurture and strength.
In all of the changing circumstances of our lives,
    plant your word in our hearts again and again,
    that we might grow into the Christian disciples
       you call us to become. Amen.

PRAYER OF CONFESSION (GENESIS 25)

God of unity and peace,
    we know that we are not always a peaceful people.
Where there is conflict,
    help us to find your peace.
Where we feel envy,
    help us to know your soothing balm of acceptance.
When we are overcome with anger,
    grant us the grace of forgiving hearts.
When we have caused conflict and pain,
    forgive us.
Help us to grow as disciples of love and peace
    in all that we say and all that we do.
In the name of the Prince of Peace, we pray. Amen.

BENEDICTION (PSALM 119)

Go forth, knowing that the Word of God goes with us,
    as a lamp to our feet and a light to our paths.
Go in faith.

BENEDICTION (MATTHEW 13)

Go, bear fruit in all that you say and do.
Plant your faith in fertile soil,
    that it may be watered and nourished.
Plant God's Word in everyone you meet,
    that new faith may bloom and grow.
Plant your love all around,
    for love is the nourishment that changes lives.
Go in faith, hope, and joy,
    for you are the seeds that will change the world.

JULY 17, 2005

Ninth Sunday After Pentecost
Mary J. Scifres

COLOR
Green

SCRIPTURE READINGS
Genesis 28:10-19*a*; Psalm 139:1-12, 23-24; Romans 8:12-25;
Matthew 13:24-30, 36-43

THEME IDEAS
Jacob finds God's presence in an unexpected place and constructs an altar for worship. The psalmist finds God's presence in our very souls and proclaims it to be a wondrous thing. In Romans, Paul finds God's Spirit groaning alongside us to bring God's promises to fruition. In Matthew, Jesus promises to plant us as the seeds of God, even as Jesus reminds us that the struggle is a fragile process for the seeds and the sower. Yet in the struggle, God is there, always.

CALL TO WORSHIP (ROMANS 8)
All creation is waiting. Can you hear it?
**The groans of labor are all around,
waiting for the promises of God.**
All creation is waiting. Can you see it?
**The plantings of the Spirit are struggling to bud
and bring forth fruit.**
All creation is waiting. Can you feel it?

**The children of God are yearning for adoption
and acceptance.**
All creation is waiting. Can you believe it?
**The promises of God are here,
for we are the firstfruits of the Spirit.**
We are the adopted children of God,
**accepted and acceptable
in Christ's gracious sight.**
Come, children of God, our Father awaits our worship.
**Come, children of God,
our Mother has given us birth!**

CALL TO WORSHIP (MATTHEW 13)

Come to Christ, our living vine.
**We come into Christ's presence,
filled with the possibility of new life.**
Be planted in fertile soil,
deep and rich with God's promise.
**We welcome God's growth
in times of transition and change.**
Open your hearts and minds to the Spirit
that nurtures and sustains us.
**We open our lives to the One
who calls us to worship.**

CONTEMPORARY GATHERING WORDS (GENESIS 28)

How awesome is this place,
none other than the house of God!
You are awesome in this place, mighty God!
How awesome is this place,
none other than the gate of heaven!
You are awesome in this place, mighty God!

PRAISE SENTENCES (GENESIS 28)

Surely the presence of the Lord is in this place!
Surely God is with us now!

Surely the presence of the Lord is in this place!
Surely God is with us now!

OPENING PRAYER (PSALM 139)
Wonderful God,
    you have searched me and known me.
Set me on my path this day.
Guide me in your ways.
Lead me in your paths
    of everlasting love and life. Amen.

OPENING PRAYER (MATTHEW 13)
Loving God,
    we thank you for all those
        who have planted your word
            and grown in faith before us.
Bless us in our ministries of service and word.
Guide us as your church.
Plant your word in our hearts
    and your faith in our lives,
        that we might carry your message of love and hope
        to a world in need.
Nurture us with your Spirit,
    that we might grow into a strong and mighty forest
        of faithful discipleship.
Live in us,
    that we might be your people
        and honor your holy name.
By the grace and love of Christ Jesus, we pray. Amen.

PRAYER (PSALM 139)
O God,
    you have searched my every thought
        and you know my very being.
You are with me,
    no matter how far I run
        or how long I wander.

You are beside me in my darkest hours
    and on my brightest days.
If I could fly to the ends of the earth,
    you would fly alongside me.
If I delve in the deepest of sins,
    you are there.
If I reach for the highest goal,
    you are there.
In all of life,
    good and bad, sorrow and joy,
    faith and doubt, courage and fear,
    you walk with me, Companion God.
Blessed be! Amen.

BENEDICTION (GENESIS 28)

Surely God is in this place,
living among us now.
Surely God goes with us now,
into a world of woe.
Take God's promises and steadfast love,
Gifts for all of God's precious world.
Go from these gates of heaven
and take heaven into the world.

BENEDICTION (MATTHEW 13)

Go forth, good seeds of this world.
Guard God's promises well,
    that you may be planted in fertile soil!
Harvest with love and grace,
    that your gifts may be blessings to all!

JULY 24, 2005

Tenth Sunday After Pentecost
Joanne Carlson Brown

COLOR
Green

SCRIPTURE READINGS
Genesis 29:15-28; Psalm 105:1-11, 45*b*; Romans 8:26-39; Matthew 13:31-33, 44-52

THEME IDEAS
In the midst of summer, when our thoughts seem occupied with relaxation and fun, we find ourselves confronted with the difficult task of faithful living. Today's texts abound with hard work and treachery and puzzling images of the kingdom God. Yet these texts are tempered with deep love, love of another person and of God. These texts help us to see that no matter what happens in our lives nothing can separate us from the love of God.

CALL TO WORSHIP (PSALM 105)
Give thanks to God and call on God's name.
Sing to God; sing praises to God!
Make known God's deeds among the people.
Sing to God; sing praises to God!
Seek God's presence and God's strength.
Sing to God; sing praises to God!
Let us worship our God, for God is faithful.

CALL TO WORSHIP (MATTHEW 13)
Come and worship God with your whole heart.
We come as mustard seeds of faith.
Come and worship God with your whole being.
We come as leaven for the world.
Come and worship God with your whole mind.
**We come as treasures and pearls of great price,
enriching the world with our witness.**
Come and worship God with your whole lives.

CONTEMPORARY GATHERING WORDS (ROMANS 8)
Come with confidence before our God.
For nothing can separate us from the love of God.
Can hunger?
No!
Can hardship?
No!
Can people who are against us?
No!
Can death?
No!
Can anything in all creation?
No!
Then let us worship this most amazing God.

PRAISE SENTENCES (PSALM 105)
Give thanks to God and call on God's name.
God has done wonderful works for us.
God's promises are sure.
Sing to God, sing praises to God!
Praise our God!

PRAISE SENTENCES (ROMANS 8)
The Spirit intercedes for us with sighs too deep for words.
We know all things work together
for those who love God.

Because God is for us, none can be against us.
Nothing, absolutely nothing, can separate us
  from the love of God.

OPENING PRAYER (ROMANS 8, PSALM 105)

Our gracious and ever loving God,
  we come in the midst of summer
    looking for refreshment.
We rest in the knowledge
  of the wonderful works you have done for us,
  and of the deep and abiding love you have for us
    and for all God's people.
Search our hearts.
Fill our soul with your indwelling Spirit
  who whispers to our soul
    that all will be well if we but trust in you.
Shine your light before us,
  that we may see our path to you
    and to your kingdom on earth. Amen.

PRAYER OF CONFESSION (GENESIS 29, MATTHEW 13)

We pause this morning, O God,
  with heavy hearts.
We live in the midst of great and abiding love,
  but also in the midst of deceit and lies.
May we be found faithful in all we do.
May we speak the truth in love
  and live lives of love each day.
Too often we seek you in the spectacular
  and otherworldly.
May we see the many inbreakings of your kingdom
  in the everyday, ordinary things of life:
    in mustard seeds, yeast,
      treasures in fields, and fish gathered in nets.
May we be able to answer with a full-throated yes
  when asked if we have understood your teachings
    and your call. Amen.

WORDS OF ASSURANCE (ROMANS 8)

When we are not sure how to pray,
    or if we are even able to address God in prayer,
    the Spirit intercedes for us
    with sighs too deep for words.
Know that no matter what, nothing,
    absolutely nothing can ever separate us
    from God's presence and God's love.

BENEDICTION

With a song of praise on our lips,
    we go forth with God.
With the love of God in our hearts,
    we go forth with God.
With a commitment to usher in God's kingdom,
    we go forth with God.
With all that we are and all we can be,
    we go forth with God.

JULY 31, 2005

Eleventh Sunday After Pentecost

B. J. Beu

COLOR
Green

SCRIPTURE READINGS
Genesis 32:22-31; Psalm 17:1-7, 15; Romans 9:1-5; Matthew 14:13-21

THEME IDEAS
Doubt, faith, and blessing are powerfully interwoven in the above scripture readings. Jacob doubts he can cross Esau's land without being attacked, so he sends his family and flocks ahead. When confronted by an angel, Jacob is not cowed by his earlier lack of faith but demands to be blessed. Paul has no doubt that God has called him to preach to the Gentiles, yet it does not negate the blessings God has bestowed upon Israel. And while Jesus' disciples want to send the crowds away for food, Jesus knows that they themselves could bless the hungry followers with food, if they had sufficient faith. Even in our doubts, blessings are to be had to those who seek them with faith in the One who blesses us.

CALL TO WORSHIP (PSALM 17)
O Lord, we long to be like the psalmist,
  with lips free of deceit

and no wickedness in our mouths.
Give us the self-confidence that comes from godly living,
avoiding the ways of the violent,
and keeping our feet firmly held to your paths.
Show us your steadfast love.
Be our savior,
a refuge from our adversaries.
Let us behold your face in righteousness.
Let us behold your likeness,
and we shall be satisfied.

CALL TO WORSHIP (GENESIS 32)

Even when our faith falters, O Lord,
we will not let you go.
Even when we are bruised by this world of yours, O God,
we will not let you go.
Now, more than ever, O Lord, we need a blessing;
we will not let you go.
Bless your people, O God, as you blessed Jacob before us.

CONTEMPORARY GATHERING WORDS (MATTHEW 14)

My people are hungry, give them something to eat.
There are too many of them.
My people are hungry, give them something to eat.
We have only five loaves and two fish.
My people are hungry, give them something to eat.
How can it be enough?
With God, all things are possible.
Thanks be to God!

PRAISE SENTENCES

Praise God who fills us with glory.
Praise God who has adopted us into Christ's family.
Praise God who gives us the Book of Life.
Praise God who wills our hearts with worship.
Praise God who gives us the Messiah.

OPENING PRAYER (GENESIS 32)

Eternal God,
in the midst of our fears and doubts,
you call us home.
Be with us on our journey when our faith wavers
and we seek safety in our own clever schemes.
Stay with us when we have need of you, O God,
and bless us in our struggles,
that we might be a blessing for others. Amen.

OPENING PRAYER (MATTHEW 14)

God of mystery and power,
teach us to be like Jesus.
When we are weary,
give us the courage to take time apart
and gather our strength.
When we return,
grant us the courage to seek the welfare of others
and see the best in one another.
When we are faced with those in need,
help us reach out in compassion,
that the world might know
that we are your disciples.
In Jesus' name we pray. Amen.

OFFERTORY PRAYER

Holy God, all that you have given us is yours.
Help those of us with means
reach out to those in need.
Teach us the joy
that comes from sharing our abundance
with those who live in want.
May we open our hearts, like Jesus,
that the world may be fed
and made whole. Amen.

BENEDICTION (PSALM 17)

The love of God is wonderful.
O God, shower us with your steadfast love.
God is our refuge and strength.
Be with us as we leave this place, O God,
and shelter us from all harm.
Behold God's face in righteousness.
We will behold God's likeness,
and be a people of peace.

BENEDICTION

Go forth with the blessing of God,
who seeks to bring you through hostile lands
to a land flowing with milk and honey.
Go with the blessings of the One
who heals our wounds and makes us whole.

AUGUST 7, 2005
Twelfth Sunday After Pentecost
Lawrence Wik

COLOR
Green

SCRIPTURE READINGS
Genesis 37:1-4, 12-28; Psalm 105:1-6, 16-22, 45*b*; Romans 10:5-15; Matthew 14:22-33

THEME IDEAS
Each of the day's readings deals with the theme of deliverance. In Genesis 37, Joseph's initial deliverance from death to slavery in Egypt is but a precursor to God's deliverance of Israel from famine, a theme picked up in Psalm 105. In Romans 10, God's deliverance is available to all who call on the name of Jesus Christ, who confess him with their lips, and who believe in him with their whole heart. Matthew 14 recounts Peter walking on the water, the saving power of faith, and Jesus' willingness to deliver us even when we falter in fear and doubt.

CALL TO WORSHIP (GENESIS 37, PSALM 105, ROMANS 10, MATTHEW 14)
The Word of the Lord is calling us.
**God, we see you living in our dreams
and know that you are with us.**

The Word of the Lord is testing us.
God, we hear you in the storms of life
and know that you will save us.
The Word of the Lord is near to us.
God, we speak of you with faithful lips
and know that you are in our hearts.
The Word of the Lord has come to deliver us.
God, we praise you for your righteousness
and call upon your name.

CALL TO WORSHIP (PSALM 105)

We call upon your name, O Lord.
O ruler of all people, set us free!
We seek you and your strength, O Lord.
O ruler of all people, set us free!
We hunger for new life, O Lord.
O ruler of all people, set us free!
We pray for hearts of praise, O Lord.
O ruler of all people, set us free! Come!
Make known in us your mighty deeds.

CONTEMPORARY GATHERING WORDS (MATTHEW 14)

Lord, if it is you, come calm our fears.
Take heart, be not afraid, for God is here.
Lord, if it is you, please bid us·come.
Come, reach out, for God is near at hand.
Lord, if it is you, increase our faith.
Walk with strength, dismiss life's storms,
and hold the hand of grace.

CONTEMPORARY GATHERING WORDS (ROMANS 10)

Like the air we breathe,
God is near.
Like the words we speak,

God is near.
Like the hope we were taught
from the love Jesus brought,
God is near.
Like a song in our heart,
God is near!

PRAISE SENTENCES (PSALM 105)
Give thanks to the Lord!
Sing to the Lord!
Glorify God's holy name!
Our God is wonderful! (B. J. Beu)

UNISON PRAYER (GENESIS 37, ROMANS 10)
Eternal God,
    when others see your love for us
    and how we are set apart,
    they often do not speak peaceably to us.
When others hear the dreams
    you have planted within us,
    they often cannot speak peaceably to us.
When others experience
    how you transform our misfortunes
    into works for good,
    they often will not speak peaceably to us.
But we pray someday that they will speak peace
    and be restored in love.
Make us beautiful and humble, God,
    to bear the good news of your peace. Amen.

OPENING PRAYER (PSALM 105)
God, make known to us all you have done,
    and all you have yet to do.
Speak to us once more
    your powerful message of deliverance—
        deliverance from oppression and injustice,

167

deliverance from fear and hopelessness,
deliverance from slavery to sin and death.
Free us in this hour from all that would stifle our spirits.
May your word in us bear fruit for all the world.

PRAYER OF CONFESSION (MATTHEW 14)

God, how easy it is for us
to shy away from being faithful!
There is so much tumult in our lives,
so much uncertainty.
When you come to us in an opportunity,
we are fearful, and we cry out our resistance.
When you call us forward to life,
we see only the difficulties and trials in store for us.
We forget that your hand
is ever ready to save and preserve us.
God, forgive us our fears and doubts,
and free us to walk boldly in faith.
In the name of the One who leads us to life we pray.
Amen.

BENEDICTION (PSALM 105)

Seek the Lord and the strength God has to give.
Look for God's presence continually.
Live faithfully, remembering all that God has done.
And be ever mindful of God's promises.
The Lord has freed us to be fruitful.
We will lead lives of service and praise.

BENEDICTION (GENESIS 37)

Our brothers are suffering injustice
and are in need of deliverance.
"Come," says God, "I will send you to them."
Here we are, Lord.
We will go and seek our brothers.
Our sisters are suffering abuse,

and are in need of deliverance.
"Come," says God, "I will send you to them."
Here we are, Lord.
We will go and seek our sisters.
Though the way is fraught with peril,
God will go with us
and work to redeem suffering in our midst.
Here we are, Lord!
We will go in the power of your love!

AUGUST 14, 2005

Thirteenth Sunday After Pentecost
Kevin C. Bogan

COLOR
Green

SCRIPTURE READINGS
Genesis 45:1-15; Psalm 133; Romans 11:1-2*a*, 29-32; Matthew 15:(10-20) 21-28

THEME IDEAS
Unity and reconciliation are fundamental themes in the story of Joseph's acceptance and forgiveness of his brothers. Unity is also a central theme in Psalm 133. We are called to be one with, and reconciled to, all those in our world, regardless of race, creed, color, or religious belief. Matthew's Gospel gives us an insight into the persistent faith that overcomes barriers in relationships and that reconciles us to others who may be unlike us.

CALL TO WORSHIP (PSALM 133)
How good it is to live together in unity
  and join our hearts and minds in one accord.
How wonderful it is to gather as Christ's disciples
  and be in the presence of God.
Before the very rocks cry out,
  **let us sing God's praises and witness to our faith
  in our Savior, Jesus Christ.**

CALL TO WORSHIP (GENESIS 45, MATTHEW 15)
From the ends of the earth we have gathered,
  people of every tribe and every nation,
with like minds and hearts,
  **but with different careers, backgrounds
  and interests.**
Shape us to be your body as we set aside our differences
and embrace our common purpose,
  to worship you in one mind and in one spirit.

CONTEMPORARY GATHERING WORDS (GENESIS 45)
God has gathered us together
  for such a time as this.
We have been called to fill this place
with praise and worship
  for such a time as this.
May we be filled with God's glory and grace
  for such a time as this.
Let us lift the name of the Lord
  for such a time as this.

PRAISE SENTENCES (PSALM 133)
How good and pleasant it is
  when Christians live together in unity!
Because of God's love we have been formed into a family
  that transcends time and space.
Praise God for the inheritance of grace and mercy
  that we have received as children of God.

OPENING PRAYER (MATTHEW 15)
Gracious God of the universe,
  you have called us here from different walks of life.
From our diverse backgrounds,
  you have knit us into a unified family of faith.
We pray that, even as you have accepted us as we are,

we can learn to accept others
whose ways are different from our own.
As we open our hearts to you,
show us the way to open our hearts to others.
In your presence today, O God,
may we worship together without exclusion
and rejoice together without ceasing. Amen.

OPENING PRAYER (GENESIS 45)

Our most gracious God,
we humbly enter your presence this morning.
In our brokenness,
we may feel unworthy to be called your children,
yet we rejoice knowing that you have chosen us
to be your own.
We feel the warmth of your embrace as you gather us.
Though once separated from you through sin,
you have reconciled us into a family
through your forgiveness and mercy.
Help us to be a reflection of your acceptance and grace.
In the name of Christ, our Savior, we pray. Amen.

PRAYER OF CONFESSION (ROMANS 11)

Through the journey of our lives,
we confess that we have turned from your ways,
O Lord.
We have been filled with pride
and have been disobedient.
Our eyes look inward instead of outward
to the needs of those with whom we share our world.
Grant us your wisdom to see the needs of others
and the ability to reconcile our wants
with your purposes.
May your mercy flow abundantly to us and through us
as we long to be one with you.
In the name of the One

who gave us the pathway to salvation,
Jesus Christ. Amen.

BENEDICTION (PSALM 133)

Even as we have gathered together as God's family,
let us leave this place knowing that the bonds
of holy love keep us bound together.
May Christ's love so flow through us
that the world will know we are one
through the Holy Spirit.

BENEDICTION (MATTHEW 15)

Let us leave this place with open arms
ready to embrace all those in our world.
In the mission fields of our lives,
let us welcome those of all races, creeds, and colors
to the joy of the Lord in Christ Jesus.
Go forth in the name of the One who accepts us
and shows us the way of acceptance. Amen.

AUGUST 21, 2005

Fourteenth Sunday After Pentecost
Mary J. Scifres

COLOR
Green

SCRIPTURE READINGS
Exodus 1:8–2:10; Psalm 124; Romans 12:1-8;
Matthew 16:13-20

THEME IDEAS
Today's readings highlight faithful ministries. The courage of the many women who brought Moses safely to his adulthood is undergirded by their constant willingness to use their gifts to minister to and for the male children of Israel. Paul's call to present our lives as gifts to God and to recognize our different talents of equal value encourages us to utilize our ministry abilities in service to God and to the world. Finally, Jesus' challenge to Peter to become a foundational leader in the church is an awesome reminder of the power inherent in answering Christ's call to ministry.

CALL TO WORSHIP (ROMANS 12)
Offer yourselves as gifts to God this day.
We offer God our time, talent, and treasure.
Offer your lives as gifts to God throughout the week.
We offer our lives to the One who gives us life.

Offer your ministry as gifts to God's world.
We offer our ministry in service to Christ.
Offer yourselves as gifts to God.
We offer God our time, talent, and treasure.

CALL TO WORSHIP (PSALM 124)

If it had not been the LORD who was on our side
when the enemies attacked, let the people say—
If it had not been the LORD who was on our side,
we would have been swallowed up!
The flood would have swept us away.
The raging waters would have gone over us!
Blessed be the LORD,
who made heaven and earth!
Blessed be the LORD,
who is our help!
Blessed be the LORD,
for God is on our side!

CONTEMPORARY GATHERING WORDS (MATTHEW 16)

Jesus asked his disciples, "Who do you say that I am?"
In the din of this world's many answers, Jesus asks still,
"Who do you say that I am?"
"You are the Messiah, the Son of the living God!"
Christ is the Messiah, the Son of the living God!
Christ is the Messiah, the Son of the living God!
Christ is the Messiah, the Son of the living God!
Christ is the Messiah, the Son of the living God!
Thanks be to God!

PRAISE SENTENCES (ROMANS 12)

God's grace is all around.
God gives us all that we are.
Praise God for these many gifts!

175

PRAISE SENTENCES (PSALM 124)

God is on our side. Our help is in God's name!
God is on our side. Our help is in God's name!
Blessed be the Lord, who made heaven and earth!
Blessed be the Lord, who made heaven and earth!

OPENING PRAYER (ROMANS 12)

Loving God,
we offer you our lives and our gifts.
Transform us, O God,
that we may make this commitment anew
every minute of every day.
Help us to know your grace,
that we may trust in your perfect goodness.
Help us to live as your children,
that we may be the body of Christ on this earth.
Help us to answer your call,
that we may serve you in all that we say and do.
In Christ's name, we pray. Amen.

OPENING PRAYER (PSALM 124)

God of power and might,
thank you for bringing us safe thus far.
Thank you for calling us
to be bearers of goodness and truth,
justice and love.
Thank you for being our constant help and our salvation.
Thank you for being our rock and our redeemer.
Thank you for calling us to be your people,
a people of love and mercy.
In your gracious name, we pray. Amen.

BENEDICTION (EXODUS 1)

Go with the courage of the midwives.
Go with the love of Moses' mother.
Go with the boldness of Miriam, Moses' sister.

Go with the call of God in your hearts,
    a call as big and as powerful as the call of Moses.
Go in love, for you are the people of God!

BENEDICTION (PSALM 124, MATTHEW 16)

Our help is in the name of the Lord,
who made heaven and earth.
God's help will lead us on into a world of need.
Our strength is in the power of God,
who encourages us forward.
**God's strength will move us forward
into a changing world.**
Our love is by the mercy of Christ,
who loved us best.
**Christ's love will grace our lives
so that we may love this world of God.**
Amen and amen.

AUGUST 28, 2005

Fifteenth Sunday After Pentecost
John A. Brewer

COLOR
Green

SCRIPTURE READINGS
Exodus 3:1-15; Psalm 105:1-6, 23-26, 45c; Romans 12:9-21; Matthew 16:21-28

THEME IDEAS
Themes abound in today's scriptures: God calls people to ministry, not to volunteerism; serving God inevitably involves some cost to the servant; discipleship always leads to new life for the disciple and for those served; the realities of life include both good and evil. From Christ we can learn to do good in the great hope and great commission of overcoming the evil that brings harm to God's people. In most communities, the summer season of vacations and holidays is coming to an end. Anxiety and anticipation are part of getting back into the routines of the fall schedule. These texts lend themselves to thoughts and actions: God's call to serve in the midst of the fall schedule.

CALL TO WORSHIP (PSALM 105)
O, give thanks to the Lord. Call on God's name.
Make known God's deeds among the peoples.
Sing praises to the Lord. Tell of God's wonderful works.

Glory in God's holy name.
Let the hearts of those who seek the Lord rejoice.
Seek the Lord.
Seek God's strength and presence continually.
Remember the wonderful works the Lord has done.
God's miracles and judgments are sure.

CALL TO WORSHIP (ROMANS 12)

Let love be genuine; hate what is evil.
Hold fast to what is good.
Love one another with mutual affection.
Outdo one another in showing honor.
Do not lag in zeal; be ardent in spirit; serve the Lord.
Rejoice in hope. Be patient in suffering.
Persevere in prayer.
Contribute to the needs of the saints.
Extend hospitality to strangers.
Do not be overcome by evil,
but overcome evil with good.

CALL TO WORSHIP (MATTHEW 16)

Come, let us search together for our very own lives.
Let us be willing to lose our very own lives.
Come, let us search together for our very own lives.
Let us follow together, this Jesus the Christ.
How will we ever find our own lives?
Let us save our own lives
by losing them in discipleship to Christ.
Come, let us rejoice and sing
as we learn from Jesus the teacher.
For when we are lost in Christ,
we have found our very own lives.

PRAISE SENTENCES

God has set us free from all bondage!
Christ has called us to partnership in ministry!
Praise God for the wonderful works he has done!

PRAISE SENTENCES
Jesus Christ is the one who gives life!
We find new life in our walk with Christ!
Rejoice in the God who has redeemed us!
God is able to rescue us from all evil!

OPENING PRAYER (EXODUS 3, PSALM 105, ROMANS 12, MATTHEW 16)
O Lord, our Lord,
how majestic is your name in all the earth!
We come before you today
seeking freedom from our selfishness and limited views
of faith and service.
Deliver us from the kind of thinking
that excludes ourselves
from your works of salvation and healing.
Speak to us today,
as you did to Moses from the burning bush,
and let us know your strength to fulfill the ministry
you give to us. Amen.

OPENING PRAYER (EXODUS 3, PSALM 105, ROMANS 12, MATTHEW 16)
God of all seasons,
come to us anew on this Sunday morning.
As we feel the changing pace of our common lives,
let us know again the wonder of your ordered world
and your wonderful desires for our fulfillment.
We come before you with both anxiety and hope.
As we sing and pray,
remove our fears and insecurities
and give us the assurance of things hoped for,
the evidence of things not seen. Amen.

PRAYER OF CONFESSION

God of mercy and grace,
  we bow before you in humility,
  knowing all too well our sinful resistance
    to your will and leadership.
Forgive us for holding so tightly to our own ways
  that we fail to discover the wonderful life
    available to us in Jesus Christ.
Forgive us when we have been part of the problem
  rather than part of the salvation
  you offer to your people.
We are sorry.
Give us the love
  that will enable us to bring good, not evil,
  to those around us. Amen.

BENEDICTION

The God who redeemed the Hebrew people in Egypt
  continues to redeem people who suffer evil today.
May the God of redeeming love be with us
  as we engage our world
  with the transforming power of Christ.
Let us hold fast to the faith that perseveres
  and overcomes evil with good.
It is in the name of Christ Jesus that we go forth
  to serve in ministry and mission. Amen.

BENEDICTION

Receive now this word of blessing:
  God will speak to you from a burning bush,
  or in the quiet moments of your week.
God wishes good for you. God calls you for good.
Go forth knowing that, in Christ, you are never alone!

SEPTEMBER 4, 2005

Sixteenth Sunday After Pentecost

B. J. Beu

COLOR

Green

SCRIPTURE READINGS

Exodus 12:1-14; Psalm 149; Romans 13:8-14; Matthew 18:15-20

THEME IDEAS

Love and judgment are the two themes that dominate today's readings. Out of love for the Hebrew people, God promises to execute judgment against the Egyptians for enslaving God's people. Exodus commands us to observe and celebrate a day of remembrance, to commemorate the sparing of the Hebrew firstborn children from death. The psalmist exhorts us to sing praises for God's judgment against unjust rulers. The epistle reading calls us to judge our own conduct, give up sinful living, and live as children of the light. Finally, the Gospel reading offers us a road map on how to deal with conflict and grievances within the church. Here, acts of judgment are intended to reforge the bonds of love between the estranged parties.

September 4, 2005

CALL TO WORSHIP (PSALM 149)

Praise the Lord!
Sing to the Lord a new song.
Praise God in the assembly of the faithful.
Let all God's children rejoice in their king.
Praise the Lord with dancing.
Praise God's name with tambourine and lyre.
Let the faithful exult in glory.
The Lord executes vengeance on the nations.
God decrees judgment on unjust leaders.
Praise the Lord!

CALL TO WORSHIP (ROMANS 13)

Love one another as you have been loved by God.
Love has brought us here.
All the commandments are summed up in this word:
"Love your neighbor as yourself."
Love has brought us here.
Put on Christ Jesus and fulfill the law of love.
Love has brought us here.

CONTEMPORARY GATHERING WORDS (EXODUS 12)

Gather the people. Declare a feast.
God's salvation is at hand.
Put aside all quarrels and arguments.
God's salvation is at hand.
Place your trust in God, who delivers us from death.
God's salvation is at hand.
Gather the people. Declare a feast.
God's salvation is at hand.

PRAISE SENTENCES (PSALM 149)

Praise the Lord! Sing to the Lord a new song.
Praise God with dance, with drums and guitar.
Praise the Lord! Sing to the Lord a new song.

Rejoice in our God! Give glory to God's holy name.
Praise the Lord! Sing to the Lord a new song.

OPENING PRAYER OR PRAYER OF CONFESSION (ROMANS 13)

God of holy light,
   come to us in the midst of our gloom and despair.
Teach us to lay aside the works of darkness
   and put on the armor of light.
Help us to love one another,
   even as you have loved us.
Help us follow Jesus' commandment
   to love our neighbor
      as we love ourselves.
Bring us into the light of your morning,
   that we may wake from the darkness of ignorance,
   and put on Christ Jesus,
      who leads us to fullness of life. Amen.

OPENING PRAYER (EXODUS 12)

Eternal God,
   when your people in Egypt cried out in bondage,
      you remembered your promise to Abraham and Sarah
         and came to their rescue.
Remember us also, O God, when we are in need.
Come to our aid with a mighty hand and outstretched arm,
   that we might be delivered from our bondage
      to sin and death.
We ask this in the name of your Son, Jesus Christ,
   who is the Lord of life. Amen.

PRAYER OF CONFESSION (ROMANS 13, MATTHEW 18)

Loving God,
   you have taught us that in loving one another,
   we fulfill the law and all the commandments.
Try as we may,

we have not always loved our neighbor
  as we have loved ourselves.
When others have wronged us,
  we have not always kept the offense to ourselves
    or sought to mend the breach in private.
We prefer the role of victim,
  over the role of reconciler.
Help us reach out in love,
  that the church might be a place of healing,
  in Jesus' name. Amen.

ASSURANCE OF PARDON (ROMANS 13)

The God who raised Jesus from the dead
  is here to waken us from our sleep,
  and gird us with the armor of light.
Put on Christ Jesus and you will be saved,
  you will be children of light and love.

BENEDICTION (PSALM 149)

Sing to the Lord a new song.
  God has put a new song in our hearts.
Rejoice in the Lord, who brings us victory.
  God has put a victory song in our hearts.
Go with blessings of God, who brings us victory.
  We go with God's song in our hearts.

BENEDICTION (MATTHEW 18)

Go with the love of God,
the blessings of our Lord Jesus Christ,
and the joy of the Holy Spirit.
  We go forth as God's people,
  redeemed and made whole.
Go forth together, as the body of Christ.
  We go forth with Christ,
  remembering that wherever we are,
  God is with us when we gather
  in Christ's name.

SEPTEMBER 11, 2005

Seventeenth Sunday After Pentecost
Mary J. Scifres

COLOR
Green

SCRIPTURE READINGS
Exodus 14:19-31; Exodus 15:1*b*-11, 20-21; Romans 14:1-12;
Matthew 18:21-35

THEME IDEAS
These readings fall into separate thematic categories. The
Exodus readings focus on the majesty and saving power of
God, recounting perhaps the most significant event in the
Hebrew Scriptures: the Israelites' escape from Egypt across
the sea. The New Testament readings focus on the human
temptation to judge others while Christ calls us to forgive. In
Romans, Paul charges Christians to focus on living for Christ
and accepting one another in our different stages of faith. In
Matthew, Jesus warns of the judgment one can expect when
one withholds forgiveness and grace from others.

CALL TO WORSHIP (EXODUS 14, EXODUS 15)
Sing to the Lord of power and might.
    God is our salvation and strength.
Praise the God of our ancestors.
    The Lord is glorious in power.
Exalt the One who loves us and saves us.

Our God is full of majesty and splendor.
Sing to the Lord of power and might.
Our God is an awesome God.

CALL TO WORSHIP (ROMANS 14)

God has called us here.
We come in answer to Christ.
God welcomes us all.
We come with trusting faith.
God will bless us now.
We come in hope and joy.

CONTEMPORARY GATHERING WORDS (EXODUS 15)

Come into the awesome presence of God.
We'll sing to the Lord!
Come into the loving grace of Christ.
We'll sing to the Lord!
Come into the mighty power of God's Spirit.
We'll sing to the Lord!

CONTEMPORARY GATHERING WORDS (ROMANS 14)

Welcome, all who gather here.
Welcome, you who are weak in faith.
Welcome, you who know of God's love.
Welcome, all who gather here, for God is with us now!

PRAISE SENTENCES (EXODUS 15)

Sing to the Lord, who triumphs over the powers of evil.
Sing to the Lord of might!
Sing to the Lord of might!
Praise God, awesome and wonderful!
Praise God who is with us now!
Praise God who is with us now!

OPENING PRAYER (EXODUS 14)

God of love and God of power,
  be with us in this hour.
Turn back the sea of worry and doubt
    that prevents us from entering into your presence.
Hold back the tides of temptation
    that would sweep over us and lead us away from you.
Divide the waters
    that keep us from crossing over
      to your promised land.
Cover us with a cloud of love
    that we might be your people.
Shine in front of us like a pillar of fire
    that we might walk in your ways.
Stretch out your hand to create a path of dry land
    that we might follow where you lead.
In your mighty name, we pray. Amen.

OPENING PRAYER (ROMANS 14, MATTHEW 18)

Loving God,
  welcome us into your house of worship.
Help us to know your acceptance and your grace
    as we worship you.
Fill us with your grace and mercy,
    that others may find us to be
      generous and loving friends.
In Christ's name, we pray. Amen.

PRAYER OF CONFESSION (EXODUS 14)

God of power and might,
    save us from the things that would drown us.
Rescue us from the depths of despair
      when we run into the quicksand of harried lives
        and selfish attitudes.
Transform our anger into mercy
      when we seek to pursue our enemies with vengeance.

Shine upon us like a pillar of light,
    when we walk in darkness.
Remind us of your promises and your calling in our lives
    when we forget that we are your people.
Hold back the waters that threaten us.
Forgive our many wrong turns and pointless pursuits.
Love us into blessedness,
        that we may be your people
            and you may be our God,
            today and all days. Amen.

PRAYER OF CONFESSION (ROMANS 14, MATTHEW 18)

God of mercy and grace,
    forgive us for our judgmental ways
        and help us to remember your grace.
When we hold back our forgiveness from others,
    loosen the chains of our resentment
        and open us to mercy and love.
Forgive us, gracious God,
    even as we strive to forgive others.
Amen.

WORDS OF ASSURANCE (EXODUS 15)

Sing to the Lord, for God has triumphed gloriously.
God has thrown all of our sins and shortcomings
into the sea of forgiveness and grace.

WORDS OF ASSURANCE (ROMANS 14)

We do not live to ourselves,
    and we do not die to ourselves.
If we live, we live to the Lord, and if we die,
    we die to the Lord.
So then, whether we live or whether we die,
    we are the Lord's.
As God's people,

we are forgiven in the name of Jesus Christ,
who is Lord of both the dead and the living.

BENEDICTION (EXODUS 15, ROMANS 14, MATTHEW 18)

Go forth, singing to God,
    who triumphs over evil and cruelty,
    and who declares love in the midst of hate,
    and bestows grace in place of judgment.
Go forth with God's song in your heart,
    declaring love in the midst of hate,
    and grace in place of judgment.

BENEDICTION (MATTHEW 18)

We go into the world,
full of Christ's mercy and grace.
We go to share God's love,
a love of power and might.
Share Christ's love in all you do.
We'll love, by the grace of God!

SEPTEMBER 18, 2005

Eighteenth Sunday After Pentecost
Bill Hoppe

COLOR
Green

SCRIPTURE READINGS
Exodus 16:2-15; Psalm 105:1-6, 37-45; Philippians 1:21-30; Matthew 20:1-16

THEME IDEAS
God provides for all our needs. Yet at times, we find ourselves complaining about anything and everything, even the way in which God takes care of us! One month into their flight from Egypt, the Hebrews accused Moses of bringing them into the wilderness to starve them to death. Despite their grumbling, the Lord sent bread from heaven, and this manna sustained them for forty years. The laborers in Jesus' parable also complained. The laborers who had worked the longest resented receiving the same wage as those who had worked the least. But as their master pointed out, it wasn't when they were called to work that was important, it was that they were called at all—the last will be first, and the first will be last. For the apostle Paul, as long as he was still living and working, all labor was fruitful labor for God.

CALL TO WORSHIP (EXODUS 16, PSALM 105, JOHN 6)

The bread of God comes down from heaven
and gives life to the world!
Lord, give us this food that lasts forever!
Christ is this living bread from heaven!
Christ is the bread of life!
Whoever eats this bread will live forever!
Lord, give us this bread always!

CALL TO WORSHIP (PSALM 105)

Give thanks to the Lord. Call on the name of God!
Make the Lord's deeds known to all people!
Sing out; sing to God. Sing your praises to the Lord!
Sing of all God's wonderful works!
All that we need, all that we could ask for,
God gives in abundance!
Alleluia! We give thanks and praise to the Lord!

PRAISE SENTENCES (PHILIPPIANS 1)

The Lord provides all that we need!
God's love flows through our lives like a river!
The word of the Lord feeds our souls!
We stand side by side with one mind and one spirit!

OPENING PRAYER (EXODUS 16, PSALM 105)

Lord, there is no rock like you!
From you, living water flows like a river
through the desert of our souls,
bringing life to a parched and thirsty land.
Lord, there is no food that we can eat like yours.
Every word from your mouth is like bread from heaven!
You have spread your table before us.
Fill our cups with your water of life,
and satisfy our hunger with Christ,
the living bread, in whose name we pray. Amen.

September 18, 2005*

Opening Prayer (Exodus 16, Matthew 20)

You care for your people, Lord.
In the heat of the day,
  as we labor in your vineyard,
  we are covered like a cloud by your Holy Spirit.
In the dark of night,
  your fire gives us light and warmth,
  and illuminates our path.
When life's adversities well up before us
  like a great impassable sea,
  you part the angry waters
    and make us walk on solid ground.
We hunger and we thirst,
  yet you never fail to sustain us.
We are overwhelmed by your amazing love.
We humbly offer our thanks through Jesus Christ,
  in whose name we pray. Amen.

Prayer of Confession (Philippians 1)

We take you for granted, Lord.
You are with us every step of the way,
  yet we rarely think of you as a companion,
  forgetting what an honor it is just to walk with you.
We are so easily intimidated by adversity
  and by those who work against us.
How often we forget that you are always at our side,
  that none can stand against you.
Forgive us our unbelief, Lord.
In your grace,
  we have the privilege of believing in Christ,
  and of suffering for him who first suffered for us.
Holy Spirit,
  help us in our weakness and in our complacency.
Help us to live in a manner worthy of the gospel,
  that we may never take for granted
    the indescribable love of God in Christ Jesus,
    in this life and in the life to come. Amen.

September 18, 2005

193

BENEDICTION (PHILIPPIANS 1)
The harvest is plentiful.
Lord, send out laborers to your harvest!
The laborers are few.
Lord, send us out to work your harvest!
God calls us to work, to aid the harassed and helpless!
We work side by side with the Lord!
Let nothing keep us from this task!
We stand firm in Christ!

SEPTEMBER 25, 2005

Nineteenth Sunday After Pentecost
Sara Dunning Lambert

COLOR
Green

SCRIPTURE READINGS
Exodus 17:1-7; Psalm 78:1-4, 12-16; Philippians 2:1-13; Matthew 21:23-32

THEME IDEAS
In Exodus, we read of the quarreling, thirsty multitude in the wilderness and God's miracle directing Moses to strike the rock, bringing forth water. The story of the Exodus is also reflected in Psalm 78, exhorting us to recall these wonders and retell them to all generations. In the Philippians passage, Paul expresses the importance of humility and unity in Christ, reminding us in song of his obedience and glory. Matthew writes of Jesus questioning his inquisitors, who argue with each other. The parable of the two sons speaks to the rejection or acceptance of Christ. Throughout time, faithful and unfaithful alike have argued, discussed, and tested the essential nature of God. Yet, we continue to seek signs of God at work in our lives, enabling us to fulfill our promise in Christ.

CALL TO WORSHIP (EXODUS 17, PSALM 78)

Holy One, we come thirsting for the sound of your words.
May your living water fill us, O God.
Just as you led Moses to bring forth water from the rock,
Lead us this day to drink from your life-giving Spirit.
May your living water fill us, O God.
Keep us ever mindful of your wondrous deeds,
that all generations may know your glory.
May your living water fill us, O God.

CALL TO WORSHIP (PHILIPPIANS 2, MATTHEW 21)

Let us gather with Christlike humility,
obedient in his love, compassion, and sympathy.
We exalt the name of Jesus above all others.
Let us strive to honor one another more than ourselves.
We follow the example of Christ.
Let us joyfully serve in God's vineyard,
toiling without argument.
**We labor to make disciples of Christ
in all the world. Amen!**

CONTEMPORARY GATHERING WORDS (PSALM 78, PHILIPPIANS 2)

Come hear of the glorious deeds of the Lord.
God is great!
Water in the wilderness!
God is great!
A path to the Promised Land!
God is great!
A son to guide us!
God is great!
An example of humility and obedience!
God is great!

PRAISE SENTENCES (PHILIPPIANS 2)

Every tongue should confess that Jesus Christ is Lord!
Be joyful; God is at work in you today!
God gave Jesus the name that is above every name,
    that we might know his glory!

PRAISE SENTENCES (PSALM 78)

God's faithfulness endures to sustain us through Christ.
The Lord is with us in our wilderness, steadfast and strong.
Glory to God and the marvelous works of God's hands!

OPENING PRAYER (EXODUS 17, PSALM 78)

God of the wilderness,
    we seek to know your marvelous ways.
You provided water in a barren land,
    leading your people through many ordeals
        to find safety and security.
Pour out your streams of living water.
May they flow down like rivers,
    quenching our thirst for safety
        in the wilderness of our hearts.
Amen.

OPENING PRAYER (PHILIPPIANS 2)

Creator God,
    guide us with your loving hands
        as we work out our salvation in your name.
Remind us of your humble son, ever obedient,
    even to his death on the cross.
The promise of his name—
    Emmanuel, God with Us, Christ,
    Holy One, Blessed Son, Redeemer—
        resonates with us today.
Guide us in the way you would have us go,
    now and always. Amen.

PRAYER OF CONFESSION (EXODUS 17, MATTHEW 21)
Loving God,
    have patience with our quarrels, arguments, and tests.
Obedience is difficult, and humility seems complicated.
Let us be like the son who refuses you at first,
    but upon reflection comes to you willingly.
We yearn for the cleansing touch of your living waters
    that unveils your love for us.
In Christ's holy name we pray. Amen.

BENEDICTION (EXODUS 17, PSALM 78)
As we journey through life, feeling lost and alone;
    lead us out of the wilderness, Lord.
As we search for your truth, empty and dry,
    pour out your living water, Lord.
As we look for a path, struggling for a hold,
    lead us out of the wilderness, Lord.
As we follow your son, yearning for grace,
    pour out your living water, Lord. Amen!

BENEDICTION (PHILIPPIANS 2)
May the God of salvation go with you
    as you journey in humility, obedience, and love.
Amen!

OCTOBER 2, 2005

Twentieth Sunday After Pentecost/ World Communion Sunday

B. J. Beu

COLOR

Green

SCRIPTURE READINGS

Exodus 20:1-4, 7-9, 12-20; Psalm 19; Philippians 3:4b-14; Matthew 21:33-46

THEME IDEAS

The psalmist reminds us that the heavens proclaim God's glory. And despite the perfection of God's laws, we live our lives in ignorance. In Exodus, Moses presents the Hebrew people with the ten commandments, and they respond in fear. Even Paul, who walked blamelessly under the law, persecuted the church until he recognized Christ as God (Philippians). In Matthew's Gospel, Jesus tells a parable about slaves killing the master's son, as a way of foretelling his own rejection and condemnation by God's people. And yet, the heavens continue to proclaim God's glory, working together in all of creation's majesty to continually proclaim God's handiwork. We could learn much by listening to the heavens.

CALL TO WORSHIP (PSALM 19)

The heavens are telling the glory of God.
The sky proclaims the work of God's hands.
Day and night return endlessly,
showing God's steadfast love.
The sun shines upon the earth,
reflecting God's light.
The law of God is perfect, reviving the soul.
The decrees of God bring wisdom.
As we gather together,
may the words our mouths
and the meditations of our hearts
be acceptable to you, O God.
We gather together to worship the living God.

CALL TO WORSHIP (EXODUS 20)

God is calling from the mountaintop.
We wait for God's saving word.
God brings us commandments to live by,
that we may be a godly people.
We wait to be transformed by God's Word.
Worship God alone. Make no graven idols.
Do not take the Lord's name in vain.
Keep the Sabbath holy. Honor your father and mother.
We will keep God's holy commandments.
Do not murder. Be faithful to your spouse.
Do not steal or bear false witness against another.
And do not covet the things you do not have.
We will lead godly lives.

CONTEMPORARY GATHERING WORDS (MATTHEW 21)

Christ is the cornerstone that was rejected.
Christ, we build our lives upon you.
The ungodly labor and toil in vain.
Christ, we build our lives upon you.

The righteous worship the Son of the living God.
Christ, we build our lives upon you.

CONTEMPORARY GATHERING WORDS (WORLD COMMUNION)

This is the feast of God's goodness.
Let us break bread together.
This is the Sabbath of our souls.
Let us break bread together.
This is the promise of resurrection and life.
Let us break bread together.
This is the gift of Christ's love for us.
Let us break bread together.

PRAISE SENTENCES (PSALM 19)

Dance with the heavens. Sing with the stars.
Proclaim God's glory with all of creation.
God's laws are perfect and lead to life.
Dance with the heavens. Sing with the stars.
Proclaim God's glory with all of creation.

OPENING PRAYER (EXODUS 20)

God of majesty and mystery,
   we stand huddled at the base of the mountain
   as you pour forth your power and splendor.
We seek your guidance,
   but shake when you meet us face-to-face.
Bless us with your commandments,
   and teach us the ways of life and death,
   that we may be a people worthy of your loving care.
Amen.

OPENING PRAYER (MATTHEW 21)

Eternal Christ, cornerstone of our faith,
   do not abandon us when we fall away from you.

You are the true master of the vineyard,
   we are here to work in your fields,
   laboring to make disciples of all the world.
Bring us the kingdom of God,
   that we might taste of its glory
      and share your joy with the world. Amen.

PRAYER OF THANKSGIVING (WORLD COMMUNION)

God of covenant and law,
   thank you for this gift of grace,
   for this promise of salvation.
As we gather at your table and eat of this bread,
   nourish us with the truth of your word.
As we rise to go into the world,
   send us out with the hope of your salvation.
As we minister as disciples of Christ,
   remind us that we do so as one Body
      with your disciples around this great earth.
May our lives proclaim the mystery and majesty
   of your saving grace. Amen.

PRAYER OF CONFESSION (PHILIPPIANS 3)

Holy God,
   like Paul before us,
      we have failed to see your truth
         and have trusted in our own vision.
We have put our faith in our own righteousness
   rather than in the righteousness of your Son.
We have persecuted others
   out of ignorance and willful misunderstanding.
Help us forsake our pride,
   like Paul before us,
      that we might put our faith and trust in your Son,
      Jesus Christ our Lord. Amen.

ASSURANCE OF PARDON (PHILIPPIANS 3)
The One who created seeks us still,
and beckons us toward the heavenly goal
of union in Christ.
Seek God and know that our sins are forgiven.

BENEDICTION (EXODUS 20, PSALM 19)
Listen, the mountain of God thunders with good news.
God has taught us the ways of life and death.
Listen, the heavens proclaim God's glory.
God has blessed us with a world full of wonder.
Go with God.

BENEDICTION (MATTHEW 21)
Go with the blessings of the One
who was despised and rejected
and who understands
our every trial and tribulation.
Go with the blessings of the cornerstone of our faith,
Jesus Christ our Lord.

OCTOBER 9, 2005

Twenty-first Sunday After Pentecost
Joanne Carlson Brown

COLOR
Green

SCRIPTURE READINGS
Exodus 32:1-14; Psalm 106:1-6, 19-23; Philippians 4:1-9;
Matthew 22:1-14

THEME IDEAS
At first, these texts seem to have little in common. A closer
examination, however, reveals the theme of making good
and bad choices. When we try to accomplish things on our
own, or turn our back on the way that we know in our
hearts God wants us to go, we need to be reminded of who
we are and whose we are. We need to be brought back to
stand firm in God, to remember those things of timeless
value: *truth, honor, justice, purity, excellence,* and *abiding faith
and love.* Without these qualities, we cannot be the people
of God, the people whom God intends us to be.

CALL TO WORSHIP (PSALM 106)
Give thanks to God for God is good.
Praise God!
God's steadfast love endures forever.
Praise God!
Worship God with justice and righteousness.

Praise God!
Remember the mighty deeds God has done for us.
Praise God!
Let us praise God forever.
Praise God!

CALL TO WORSHIP (PHILIPPIANS 4)

Rejoice in God always!
**We come before our God with praise
and thanksgiving.**
Come worship God in peace and gentleness and love.
We come with our minds on the good gifts of God.
Rejoice in God always!

CONTEMPORARY GATHERING WORDS (EXODUS 32, PSALM 106, PHILIPPIANS 4, MATTHEW 22)

No matter who you are, come worship God.
God is faithful and just.
No matter what decisions you have made in the past,
come worship God.
God loves us fiercely with a healing, tender love.
God is calling you.
**We come with rejoicing and thanksgiving
for all God has done for us.**

PRAISE SENTENCES (PSALM 106)

Praise God! Give thanks to God who is good,
whose steadfast love endures forever.
Those who do justice and righteousness
are happy and blessed.
Take strength from the covenant and promise of God.
Remember the wonderful and mighty things
God has done for us.

PRAISE SENTENCES (PHILIPPIANS 4)

Stand firm in God with joy and love.
Rejoice in God always, again I say rejoice!

Let your gentleness and compassion be known
    to everyone.
Keep your mind on those things worthy of praise.
The peace of God will fill our hearts and minds forever.

OPENING PRAYER (MATTHEW 22)

We come this morning, O God,
    from our busy and hectic schedules.
We seem to always be too busy.
Calm our spirits.
Give peace to our souls and rest for our bodies.
May we use this time of worship to remember
    to whom we belong and what we are called to be.
Bring us in to your banquet.
May we be found clothed in garments
    of faithfulness and love.
May we accept the invitation to your banquet of love
        and justice with a full-throated, "Yes, I will come."
In the name of the One who brings us all in
    from the highways and byways of life's journeys.
Amen.

PRAYER OF CONFESSION (EXODUS 32, PSALM 106)

God, sometimes we cannot see
    what is in front of our faces.
We fail to recognize you in the things around us:
    in a beautiful sunset,
    in the brilliant color of the fall leaves,
    in the sparkling eyes of a child,
    or in the smile of an elder.
And so we despair
    and think that you have abandoned us.
Forgive us when we seek your presence on our terms—
    creating golden calves,
    gods we can manipulate and control.

For it was you who brought us out of slavery to freedom.
When we are too quick to turn aside from your ways,
    when we are a stiff-necked people,
    bring us back to your precepts.
Teach us anew who we are and whose we are,
    that we might live out your call
        to be a people of justice, mercy,
        love, and faithfulness. Amen.

WORDS OF ASSURANCE

God loves us with an unending, steadfast love.
Because of this love,
    God turns away from anger to forgiveness.
Rejoice and be glad in this promise and this reality.

BENEDICTION (PHILIPPIANS 4)

And now, the peace of God,
which surpasses all understanding,
guard your hearts and your minds in Christ Jesus.
    Amen.

BENEDICTION (PHILIPPIANS 4)

Finally, my sisters and brothers, whatever is true,
whatever is honorable, whatever is just,
whatever is pure,
whatever is pleasing, whatever is commendable,
if there is any excellence
and if there is anything worthy of praise,
think about these things
and make them come to life in your lives.
    Amen.

BENEDICTION

And now, go out to serve the God who is alive and well
and active in this world.
    **We go to live a life of faithfulness and service,
    the life to which we are called. Amen.**

OCTOBER 16, 2005

Twenty-second Sunday After Pentecost
Hans Holznagel

COLOR
Green

SCRIPTURE READINGS
Exodus 33:12-23; Psalm 99; 1 Thessalonians 1:1-10; Matthew 22:15-22

THEME IDEAS
Sometimes God does not hide. Sometimes we ask God for something and we are stunned when God answers, loud and clear. Sometimes, like Moses and Aaron and Samuel, we cry to the Lord, and God answers. Sometimes we face an obstacle, even a trap, as Jesus did before the Pharisees' smooth-talking disciples, and the right words come to us, bidden or unbidden, and it's amazing. Sometimes we are blessed to experience good news come to us, not in word only but also in power and in the Holy Spirit and with full conviction. No, the walk of faith is not always easy, and there can be long nights of doubt and distance and struggle. But, now and then there are these wonderful moments of God's yes. These, felt rarely or often, deserve celebration and thanksgiving.

CALL TO WORSHIP (PSALM 99)
["The Lord" may be substituted for "Yahweh."]
Yahweh is enthroned; Yahweh is great!

Let the peoples tremble; let the earth quake!
Yahweh is great; let the people say:
   Holy is Yahweh and greatly to be praised!
Yahweh loves justice; Yahweh forgives.
Let the people say: Holy is Yahweh!
Yahweh speaks in a pillar of cloud.
Yahweh answers those who cry.
Let us gather at the holy mountain
   and call on Yahweh's name!

CALL TO WORSHIP (EXODUS 33, PSALM 99, MATTHEW 22, 1 THESSALONIANS 1)

When God says yes,
when God doesn't hide,
   when God's glory shines,
   when God's Spirit comes,
when God sends the right words,
when God inspires us,
   when God gets us out of traps,
   when God does the very thing we ask,
may we be amazed, thankful, joyful,
and ready to say yes to God's call.
   Let us worship God!

CONTEMPORARY OPENING PRAYER (EXODUS 33, 1 THESSALONIANS 1)

O God, when you say yes,
   make us ready.
When your glory is at hand,
   let us see as much as human eyes can bear.
When your Word comes,
   make us truly thankful.
When your Spirit comes,
   make us truly joyful.
When your way is clear, O God,
   help us to follow!

CONTEMPORARY GATHERING WORDS (MATTHEW 22, 1 THESSALONIANS 1)

Teacher of courage, master of wisdom,
    revealer of the gentle and strong way, teach us!
Amaze us! Let us show the world your way!

OPENING PRAYER OR PRAYER OF CONFESSION (EXODUS 33, PSALM 99)

Dear God,
    we are not always ready to hear you say yes.
We have grown accustomed to clouded vision
    and diminished hearing.
Listening long,
    we adapt to what seems like silence.
Weathering storms,
    we drift in the calm that follows.
Waiting and watching,
    we fall asleep.
Forgive us when we miss the mark
    or miss your voice.
Rouse us gently or suddenly.
Call from afar or whisper in our ear.
Show us your will
    and help us discern how to follow,
    in Jesus' name. Amen.

BENEDICTION (EXODUS 33)

Now go forth to seek God's ways.
May you know God
    and find favor in God's sight.
May God's presence go with you
    and give you rest. Amen.

BENEDICTION (1 THESSALONIANS 1)

Become imitators of the Lord.
Receive the word with joy, inspired by the Holy Spirit.
Be disciples everywhere you go,
    that in every place your faith in God
    may become known. Amen.

OCTOBER 23, 2005

Twenty-third Sunday After Pentecost
Laura Jaquith Bartlett

COLOR
Green

SCRIPTURE READINGS
Deuteronomy 34:1-12; Psalm 90:1-6, 13-17; 1 Thessalonians 2:1-8; Matthew 22:34-46

THEME IDEAS
God cares for us, and we are called to show God's love by caring for one another! That message comes through clearly in each scripture reading. Even in the poignant story of Moses' death, we are reminded that it is God who sent Moses to rescue the Hebrews; it is God who delivered them to the Promised Land, and it is God who continues to provide after Moses is gone. Indeed, God's love has been at work in the world since the beginning of time—from everlasting to everlasting says the psalmist. So how do we respond? The epistle illustrates mutual support and nurture changing lives within the community of faith. As Jesus shows us, the requirements are very simple: Love God fully, and love our neighbors as we love ourselves.

CALL TO WORSHIP (PSALM 90)
God, we know you are with us.
From everlasting to everlasting, you are God.

You have showered your love upon all generations,
since the beginning of time.
From everlasting to everlasting, you are God.
Guide us now through this time of worship,
and into the week ahead.
From everlasting to everlasting, you are God.

CALL TO WORSHIP (1 THESSALONIANS 2)
We do not gather in vain,
for God is working in our hearts.
The love of Jesus Christ calls us together.
Our worship strengthens and empowers us
to share the gospel.
The love of Jesus Christ shines in our lives.
Proclaim the good news with boldness.
The love of Jesus Christ is at work in the world!

CONTEMPORARY GATHERING WORDS
Welcome to the house of God's love.
Is this the right time?
Is God's love available now?
God's love is always here, always ready.
But what about emergencies?
What if the system crashes?
God's love has been around since the beginning,
and it will be here after the ending.
We're ready to live in God's love, 24/7!

PRAISE SENTENCES (DEUTERONOMY 34, 1 THESSALONIANS 2)
This is the promised land of God's love!
Look around and see God's love reflected on each face.
This is a place where people are cared for and nurtured.
You are loved here.
This is the promised land of God's love!

PRAISE SENTENCES (PSALM 90, *MESSAGE*)

God, you've been our home forever.
From "once upon a time" to "kingdom come"—
    you are God!
We know you're there, God.
Surprise us with love at daybreak!
We're ready to dance in your love all day long!

OPENING PRAYER OR PRAYER OF CONFESSION

Everlasting God,
    you have been our dwelling place
        in all generations.
Since the creation of the world,
    you have nurtured us with your love.
And yet we shamefully acknowledge
    that we do not always share your love with others.
We are selective about who we choose as neighbors...
    only those who are clean,
    who look like us,
    who talk right,
    who seem safe.
Loving God,
    teach us to love you more fully.
For in loving you, our lives will show love to all others,
    even as your love encompasses all your creation,
    in all generations.
We pray in the name of your greatest gift of love,
    Jesus Christ. Amen.

OPENING PRAYER

God, you are God forever.
This alone is cause for celebration,
    but we also know that we are your people!
As we feel your love washing over us now,
may we love you with every part of our being:
    heart, mind, body, and soul.

We celebrate your love in our lives,
    and we ask for your help
        as we try our best to boldly share the good news
          of your love with others.
We pray in the name of Jesus Christ,
    who models the way for us. Amen.

BENEDICTION

Go to celebrate the God who is our home forever.
    God's love goes with us!
Go to follow Christ's example in loving God, self,
and neighbor.
    God's love goes with us!
Go with the Holy Spirit to change the world with love.
    God's love goes with us!

BENEDICTION

As you leave this place, may God's love surround you,
    uphold you, and empower you to be agents of love
    in this world. Amen.

OCTOBER 30, 2005

Twenty-fourth Sunday After Pentecost/ Reformation Sunday

Robert Blezard

COLOR

Green

SCRIPTURE READINGS

Joshua 3:7-17; Psalm 107:1-7, 33-37; 1 Thessalonians 2:9-13; Matthew 23:1-12

THEME IDEAS

Our baptism into the life of Christ recalls Israel's miraculous crossing of the river Jordan into the Promised Land. Even as baptized Christians, we sometimes wander in the wilderness of our existence, facing spiritual hunger, thirst, temptation to fall away, restlessness, and bitterness. We await God's deliverance into the promised land of intimate relationship with the divine. Such a relationship is not without work and responsibility. Paul underscores this in his letter to the Thessalonians, and Jesus warns disciples against religious complacency. But in our hard work and spiritual diligence, God's purposes undergird our lives.

CALL TO WORSHIP (JOSHUA 3, PSALM 107)

Come, let us enter the land that God has prepared for us,
God leads the way and makes our footsteps sure.

Our days of wandering in the barren desert are at an end.
God leads the way and makes our footsteps sure.
Hungry and thirsty, we cry out in deep despair.
God leads the way and makes our footsteps sure.
As in the waters of our baptism, we cross over the Jordan.
God leads the way and makes our footsteps sure.
The land is fertile and rich, with good rain in season.
God leads the way and makes our footsteps sure.
The harvest is bountiful.
We dwell in the land God has prepared for us.

CALL TO WORSHIP (PSALM 107)

Hot and weary, thirsty and hungry,
We cry to you, O God.
Seeking our true resting place,
We cry to you, O God.
As children seeking refuge,
We cry to you, O God.
Afraid and alone,
We cry to you, O God.
Longing for a home,
We cry to you, O God.
Lo! As you part the river's waters,
We cry to you, O God.
Walking across on smooth paths,
We cry to you, O God.
Secure in the home you have prepared for us,
We give you thanks, O God.

CONTEMPORARY GATHERING WORDS (PSALM 107)

Where are we going?
We are not sure. We have lost our way.
When will we get there?
We have been journeying forever.
Are we going in circles?

Sometimes it seems that way.
God says there is a place for us.
We wish we knew the way.
You just have to trust.
We will trust in the Lord.

CONTEMPORARY GATHERING WORDS (JOSHUA 3, PSALM 107)

Come! God is leading us home.
Our wandering is over at last.
Come! God is leading us home.
Home, to a safe and prosperous place.
Come! God is leading us home.
There is no more hunger or thirst.
Come! God is leading us home.
Our lives have meaning and joy.
Come! God is leading us home.
Our souls find rest at last.

PRAISE SENTENCES (JOSHUA 3, PSALM 107)

God is our deliverance!
God is our redeemer and our guide!
God's love sustains and empowers us on life's journey.
Praise God who gives us direction! Amen.

OPENING PRAYER (JOSHUA 3)

God of mercy and truth,
    through the waters of our baptism
        you have made us your own.
From the wandering wilderness of our existence,
    you lead us to the river's shore, part the waters,
    and bring us to where we can abide with you in peace.
We pray that our lives and the work of our hands
    may please you and accomplish your will for creation.
Amen.

OPENING PRAYER (PSALM 107)

God, our guide and our protector,
   as we gather today in your holy house,
   open our minds and souls and hearts,
   that we may be inclined to hear the gentle direction
      of your spirit in our lives.
Help us follow you as you lead us
   to the land you have created for us,
   where we may dwell with you and in you. Amen.

PRAYER OF CONFESSION (JOSHUA 3, PSALM 107)

Lead us home, O God,
   when we wander lost in wildernesses
      of our own making.
Like errant children,
   we stray from the safety
      of our heavenly parent.
We hear your voice calling,
   but go our own way.
We remember your teachings,
   but instead follow the foolish desires
      and whims of our hearts.
Forgive us, renew us, and lead us home,
   where we will follow your paths
      and do the work you have for us. Amen.

BENEDICTION (PSALM 107)

Go in peace!
Walk in confidence!
Follow God's leading!
Rely on God's love!
Be people of peace!

BENEDICTION (JOSHUA 3)

We leave this place by many paths.
May God be our guide.
We go in confidence that God is with us, protecting us.
May God be our guide.
May we walk in faith on paths established by God.
May God be our guide.
May we work and live with God.
May God be our guide.

NOVEMBER 1, 2005

All Saints Day
Mary J. Scifres

COLOR
White

SCRIPTURE READINGS
Revelation 7:9-17; Psalm 34:1-10, 22; 1 John 3:1-3; Matthew 5:1-12

THEME IDEAS
On this day, all people of God are challenged to be the saints of God. Life's difficulties are not ignored or downplayed in these scriptures, but comfort is assured through the love and grace of God. God's power and glory are honored, even as the sufferings of this life are recognized. In these readings, we worship God and pray for God's comfort. In these prayers, we find the hope and the faith to become the saints of God.

CALL TO WORSHIP (REVELATION 7, MATTHEW 5)
Come to the bread of life,
all who hunger for love.
Come to the living water,
all who thirst for righteousness.
Come to the shelter of God,
all who face danger and persecution.

**Come to the shade of Christ's love,
all who suffer sorrow and grief.**
Come to the Lamb of God,
all who need mercy and grace.
**Come to the Good Shepherd,
all who are poor and meek.**
We have come to bathe
in God's healing presence.
**We have come to find balm for our wounds
and comfort for our tears.**
Come let us worship God
who knows our every need.

CALL TO WORSHIP (PSALM 34)
Bless the Lord at all times.
God's praise is in our mouths.
O magnify the Lord.
We exalt God's holy name.
Seek the Lord of love.
We worship the living God.

CONTEMPORARY GATHERING WORDS (REVELATION 7)
Blessing, honor, and glory.
We praise the ancient of days.
Wisdom, power, and might.
We praise the ancient of days.
Come, we will praise together!

CONTEMPORARY GATHERING WORDS (1 JOHN 3)
We are loved by God!
Thanks be to God!
We are the children of God.
Thanks be to God!

We are invited to love one another.
Thanks be to God!
We are loved by God!
Thanks be to God!

PRAISE SENTENCES (PSALM 34)

O magnify the Lord,
Who is worthy to be praised!
O magnify the Lord,
Who is worthy to be praised!

OPENING PRAYER (1 JOHN 3, MATTHEW 5)

God of mercy and grace,
flow over us with your loving-kindness.
Help us to become the saints you call us to be.
Love us with such overwhelming abundance,
that we may love others with kindness and joy.
Bless us with your constant presence,
that we may shine with the light of your love. Amen.

OPENING PRAYER (MATTHEW 5)

Loving God, bless our time of worship.
Bless us that we might be a blessing to others.
Give us grace and mercy,
that we might bring grace and mercy
to all whom we meet.
Give us purity and humility,
that we might show Christ's example in all that we do.
Give us the hunger and thirst to bring justice
and righteousness into your world.
Give us hope and perseverance,
that we might live out your calling.
As the saints of God, we pray in Christ's holy name.
Amen.

PRAYER OF CONFESSION (MATTHEW 5, ALL SAINTS)

Being your saints is seldom easy, God.
You call us to love,
    even when we are hated.
You call us to forgive,
    even when we are condemned.
You call us to pray,
    even when we are persecuted.
Forgive us when we neglect or ignore your call.
Forgive us when we fail to be your saints.
Guide us on this journey of discipleship,
    that we may grow as your children
        and live in your love.
With faith in your mercy, we pray. Amen.

WORDS OF ASSURANCE (1 JOHN 3)

Beloved, we are the children of God!
Even when we fail, God's love never fails.
What we will be has not yet been revealed.
But we know that one day, we will be like Christ.
And until that day, we are and always will be,
    the beloved children of God.
Our sins are forgiven,
    and we are surrounded by the love of God!

BLESSING OR BENEDICTION (PSALM 34)

O taste and see that the Lord is good.
    Happy are those who take refuge in God's love.
Honor the Lord with your trust and your hope.
    Those who seek God lack for nothing.
The Lord will redeem your life.
    In God's arms of love, we are safe.
Amen and Amen.

BLESSING (REVELATION 7, MATTHEW 5)

May you know the bread of life
and the living water of Christ.
In Christ's love, may you never hunger or thirst again.
In God's protective arms,
may you find safety
from the burning difficulties of life.
In the Lamb of God's mercy,
may you find grace and forgiveness.
In the Spirit's comforting love,
may you find your tears dried
and your sorrows comforted.
In all things,
may you know that Christ is with you.
Thanks be to God!

BENEDICTION (1 JOHN 3)

Blessed are you, beloved children of God.
O, what love has been given to us!
Be a blessing to all God's children in this world.
O, what love we might give to the world!
Go forth, filled with that love in all that you do,
all that you say, and all that you are. Amen.

NOVEMBER 6, 2005

Twenty-fifth Sunday After Pentecost
Mary J. Scifres

COLOR
Green

SCRIPTURE READINGS
Joshua 24:1-3*a*, 14-25; Psalm 78:1-7; 1 Thessalonians 4:13-18; Matthew 25:1-13

THEME IDEAS
For most people who will worship with us today, servant-hood is a choice. But choosing who and what we serve varies with time and place, from day to day. Joshua and Matthew challenge us to serve God with sincerity and faithfulness. They exhort us to practice constant vigilance and to always be prepared to receive God's loving faithfulness and presence, no matter what circumstances we face.

CALL TO WORSHIP (JOSHUA 24)
Choose this day whom you shall worship.
We will worship Yahweh,
the God of our ancestors and creator of all things.
Choose this day whom you will serve.
We will serve Christ Jesus,
the Messiah and redeemer of our lives.
Choose this day whom you will praise.
We will praise the Holy Spirit, the God with us

and sustainer of our own spirits.
Come, you are welcome here.
God is present in this place.
Let us worship in spirit and truth.
Amen.

CALL TO WORSHIP OR BENEDICTION (PSALM 78)

Give ear, O people of God.
Tell of the wonders of old.
Give voice, O people of God.
Sing praises to our God.
Open your hearts, O people of God.
Live in the Spirit of God's wondrous love.
O people of God, may our lives
reflect the love we have known.

CONTEMPORARY GATHERING WORDS (1 THESSALONIANS 4)

Christ is coming soon.
We sing of the presence of God.
Christ's love is with us now.
We sing of the presence of God.
Christ Jesus will be our guide.
We sing of the presence of God.
God's presence is in this place.

CONTEMPORARY GATHERING WORDS (MATTHEW 25)

Wake up, old friends and new!
We're awake in the love of God.
Keep awake, for God is near.
We're awake in the love of God.
Prepare for the coming of Christ.
We're awake in the love of God!

PRAISE SENTENCES (JOSHUA 24, MATTHEW 25)
We choose the love of God.
We prepare for the coming of Christ.
We praise the Spirit who calls.
We are the people of God!

OPENING PRAYER (JOSHUA 24)
God of the ages, we thank you and praise you
    for leading us through the journey of life.
Lead us in this time of worship,
    that we may hear your voice and know your ways.
Be present in our worship and in our lives,
    that we may live as your people.
Guide us as we choose the course of our lives,
    that our paths may be pleasing in your sight.
In your holy name we pray. Amen.

OPENING PRAYER (JOSHUA 24)
God of our past, God of our future, be with us now.
Be present in our lives,
    that we may be present as your people in the world.
Be present in our worship,
    that we may worship and know your love.
As your people today and all days, we pray. Amen.

PRAYER (MATTHEW 25)
Gracious and loving God,
    prepare us for lives of discipleship.
When we are tired,
    enliven our spirits.
When we are forgetful,
    reawaken our senses.
When we are ill-prepared,
    give us strength to face the future.
Grant us wisdom and patience
    in these days of waiting.

Help us to live today and each day
as people who rejoice in your presence
and live as your followers. Amen.

PRAYER OF CONFESSION (MATTHEW 25)

Forgive us, Christ Jesus,
when we put you last in our lives.
Forgive us when we let our lamps burn out.
When we run too fast,
when we work too hard,
when we sleep too long,
when we stretch ourselves too thin,
forgive us and renew us.
Let your Spirit flow through our lives,
filling our lamps,
that we might shine for others in need.
In Christ's name we pray. Amen.

WORDS OF ASSURANCE (1 THESSALONIANS 4)

We have this hope: Christ is with us now and always.
Christ's kingdom will come.
Forgiveness is ours, today and all days. Amen.

BENEDICTION (MATTHEW 25)

Keep awake, for you know neither the day nor the hour.
Open your eyes, for God's presence is all around.
Open your hearts, for Christ's love is within us all.
Spread the news: Christ is coming soon!

BENEDICTION (JOSHUA 24)

Honor God in all that you do and say.
Serve God in sincerity and faithfulness.
Love God with joy and peace. Amen.

NOVEMBER 13, 2005

Twenty-sixth Sunday After Pentecost
B. J. Beu

COLOR
Green

SCRIPTURE READINGS
Judges 4:1-7; Psalm 123; 1 Thessalonians 5:1-11; Matthew 25:14-30

THEME IDEAS
Themes of judgment and redemption unify today's scripture readings. Judges recounts the familiar pattern of Israel being punished by God for falling away from God's precepts, then being rescued after repenting and returning to the Lord. The psalmist cries out for mercy to a God who hears our pleas. The epistle warns us that the day of the Lord is surely coming, but the righteous have nothing to fear if they remain vigilant and true to God. Finally, the Gospel recounts the parable of the talents and the judgment God metes out in response to our stewardship of those talents. Here, redemption comes to those who make the most of God's gifts and work for the kingdom.

CALL TO WORSHIP (PSALM 123)
We lift up our eyes, worshiping God in heaven.
Our God is wonderful to behold.
Have mercy upon us O God.

Save us from the contempt of the proud.
Fill us with your glory as we sing your praises.
Our God is wonderful to behold.

CALL TO WORSHIP (1 THESSALONIANS 5)

The night is over, day is at hand.
We will walk as children of the light.
Forsake the ways of darkness.
We will walk as children of the light.
Put on the breastplate of faith and the helmet of
salvation.
We will walk as children of the light.
Let us encourage one another and build each other up.
We will walk as children of the light.

CONTEMPORARY GATHERING WORDS (MATTHEW 25)

God has blessed you, use your gifts.
But we're afraid.
God has blessed you, use your gifts.
But others have more.
God has blessed you, use your gifts.
But will it be enough?
God has blessed you, use your gifts.
We will use our gifts. Thanks be to God.

PRAISE SENTENCES (1 THESSALONIANS 5)

Praise God, who shines light in our darkness.
Praise God, who brings victory in our defeat.
Praise God, who is the breastplate of our faith.
Praise God, who is the helmet of our salvation.
Praise God.

OPENING PRAYER OR PRAYER OF CONFESSION (MATTHEW 25)

Eternal God,
you bless us with gifts that are uniquely our own.

We have been given so much,
  yet our talents seem so small to us.
Help us shake off fear
  and boldly put our talents to use,
    that they may be a blessing to a world
      in need of your blessings.
In Christ's name we pray. Amen.

OPENING PRAYER (1 THESSALONIANS 5)

God of fall and winter, God of spring and summer,
  you know the seasons of our lives.
Let the season of darkness and sin pass away.
Lead us into the season of daylight and warmth,
  that we may be children of light.
Bless us with sober judgment,
  that we may choose to put on the breastplate of faith
    and the helmet of salvation,
    through Jesus Christ, our Lord. Amen.

BENEDICTION (1 THESSALONIANS 5)

God has not destined us for wrath
  but for salvation through our Lord Jesus Christ,
  who died for us,
  that whether we are awake or asleep
  we may live with Christ.
Therefore encourage one another and build each other up,
  and you shall be God's children.

BENEDICTION (MATTHEW 25)

God has blessed us with gifts
far more precious than jewels.
  We go with God's blessings.
God has bestowed upon us talents to change the world.
  We go with God's blessings.
God has given the gift of the Holy Spirit.
  We go with God's blessings.

NOVEMBER 20, 2005

Reign of Christ/Christ the King Sunday

Randy L. Rowland

COLOR
White or Gold

SCRIPTURE READINGS
Ezekiel 34:11-16, 20-24; Psalm 100; Ephesians 1:15-23; Matthew 25:31-46

THEME IDEAS
This is the final day of the church year: the celebration of Jesus' absolute rule over heaven and earth and the triumph of Jesus over sin, death, and evil. Praise God with exuberance. God's sovereign rule in Jesus Christ is forever. Love has conquered all. Christ's death and resurrection bring new hope and new life. God promises to watch over our lives in the grace and mercy of the King of kings. Advent pointed us to all of this—this is the foretaste of the consummation of the age when "all things" will be ordered in and by God.

CALL TO WORSHIP (PSALM 100)
Make a joyful noise to the Lord, all the earth.
Worship the Lord with gladness.
Come into God's presence with singing.

Make a joyful noise to the Lord, all you peoples!
Know that the Lord is God.
Make a joyful noise to the Lord, all the lands.
It is God who made us, and we are the Lord's.
We are God's people; the Lord is our shepherd.
Enter God's gates with thanksgiving.
Enter the Lord's courts with praise.
Give thanks to the Lord;
bless God's holy name.
For the Lord is good;
God's steadfast love endures forever.
God's faithfulness extends to all generations.

CALL TO WORSHIP (EZEKIEL 34, MATTHEW 25)

Thus says the Lord God:
I will set up one shepherd over my people.
Our shepherd will feed us
and lead us in God's ways.
Thus says the Lord God: I will save my flock.
God's flock shall no longer be ravaged.
The shepherd shall judge between the sheep
and the goats.
Thus says the Lord God: I, the Lord, will be their God!
And my servant shall be prince among them.
I, the Lord, have spoken.
Come and worship the shepherd who is king.
We come to worship and bow down
to the one shepherd.

CONTEMPORARY GATHERING WORDS (EPHESIANS 1)

We gather in God's very presence,
believing that our hearts will be enlightened.
God is among us! Christ is our king!
The power of God that raised Jesus Christ from the dead
is at work among us today.

God is among us! Christ is our king!
We come to inherit the immeasurable love and hope
that are ours in Jesus Christ.
God is among us! Christ is our king!
We worship the King.
God is among us! Christ is our king!

PRAISE SENTENCES (EPHESIANS 1)

Jesus Christ is king over all.
Christ our king shares with us his wealth of wisdom,
    power and love.
Jesus rules over the entirety of our lives,
    even our problems and struggles.
God has put all things under Christ's authority,
    and we can rest in God's goodness.
When we are empty, Jesus Christ can fill us.

PRAISE SENTENCES (MATTHEW 25)

Christ will come in glory to sort out human affairs.
Jesus Christ the king will judge the world
    with justice and mercy.
The king will say to the righteous,
    "Come, you that are blessed by my Father,
    inherit the kingdom prepared for you
    from the foundation of the world."
Jesus offers the righteous eternal life.

OPENING PRAYER (CHRIST THE KING)

Almighty God, who rules over all that is,
    by your presence among us,
    may your reign of righteousness and peace,
    joy and love, justice and mercy
        be evident in our lives.
We lift our hearts, bow our knees,
    and open our mouths to sing your praises this day.
God, we rejoice in your goodness,

and we seek the transforming power
of your love and grace.
Fill us we pray,
in the name of Christ the king,
who has conquered the forces of sin and death.
Amen.

OPENING PRAYER (PENTECOST)

God of goodness and grace,
the power of your Spirit is unleashed among us,
creating a kingdom of love and mercy
under Christ's reign.
From our Lord's infancy through his miraculous life,
humiliating death, and the triumph of his resurrection,
we marvel at your power, O God,
to bring life and love and hope to all things.
We delight in belonging to you,
and we seek to live in ways that are fresh, new, creative,
and dedicated to serving our world
in the name of Jesus Christ our Lord. Amen.

PRAYER OF CONFESSION (EZEKIEL 34)

Eternal God,
we have strayed from your paths
and cannot find our way home.
Search us, O God,
and show us both who you are
and who we are.
Pierce through the clouds and thick darkness in our lives.
Show us our sin and forgive us for our acts of darkness.
Deliver us from our arrogance and feigned strength.
Guard us in our weakness and heal our injuries,
lest in our pain, we hurt others.
Great Shepherd, cleanse us, restore us,
judge us with gentleness,
and feed us with the sustenance of your Spirit.
Enrich us with your justice.

Rule over us,
that we might find green pastures and still waters
as the sheep of your pasture
and the flock of your hand. Amen.

ASSURANCE OF PARDON (EZEKIEL 34)

Hold fast to God's words.
"I myself will search for my sheep,
and will seek them out.
As shepherds seek out their flocks
when they are among their scattered sheep,
so I will seek out my sheep.
I will rescue them from all the places
to which they have been scattered."
Through the love of our shepherd, we are forgiven.

BENEDICTION (HEBREWS 13)

Now may the God of peace,
the great Shepherd of the sheep,
and the glory of the Holy Spirit
make us complete in every good thing,
that we may do the will of God,
who blesses and keeps us from all evil.
Amen.

BENEDICTION

Peace be with you.
May Christ the King's peace be with us all.
May the love of God,
the grace of our king Jesus Christ,
and the fellowship of the Holy Spirit
be with us now and forevermore.
We go in peace to serve the Lord.
Amen.

NOVEMBER 24, 2005

Thanksgiving Day
Mary J. Scifres

COLOR
Green

SCRIPTURE READINGS
Deuteronomy 8:7-18; Psalm 65; 2 Corinthians 9:6-15; Luke 17:11-19

THEME IDEAS
God's desire for our gratitude is the common theme of this year's Thanksgiving readings. Even as the various scripture writers rehearse the many abundant gifts of God and the miraculous power of Christ Jesus, they remind us to return our thanks to God. In so doing, we multiply the blessings of God in our world.

CALL TO WORSHIP (DEUTERONOMY 8)
God has brought us good things,
gifts of life and abundance.
God calls us to remember,
to give thanks and loving praise.
We remember the God who made us,
who grants us all we need.
We worship the God who loves us,
who welcomes us and calls us here.

CALL TO WORSHIP (PSALM 65)

Awesome is our God,
who calls us into worship.
**Awesome is our God,
who establishes all the earth.**
Awesome is our God,
who delivers and saves us!
**Awesome is our God,
who makes the mountains and mighty seas.**
Awesome is our God,
who makes the evening and morning light.
**Awesome is our God,
who crowns the year with bounty.**
Awesome is our God,
who calls us into worship.
**We sing and shout for joy
as we worship our awesome God!**

CONTEMPORARY GATHERING WORDS (PSALM 65)

Praise God who answers prayers!
Our God is an awesome God!
Praise God who saves us all!
Our God is an awesome God!
Praise God who nourishes the earth!
Our God is an awesome God!
Praise God who provides for us!
Our God is an awesome God!

PRAISE SENTENCES (2 CORINTHIANS 9)

Thanks be to God, who gives us all we need!
Thanks be to God, who gives us all we need!
Thanks be to God, who gives the gift of grace!
Thanks be to God, who gives the gift of grace!

OPENING PRAYER (DEUTERONOMY 8, LUKE 17)

Gracious God,
we thank you for your many abundant gifts.

For healing and wholeness,
    we thank you.
For love and grace,
    we praise you.
For life and its fullness,
    we are ever grateful.
For this time of worship,
    we offer you our thanks and praise,
    in celebration of your many gifts.
In Jesus' name we pray. Amen.

OPENING PRAYER (2 CORINTHIANS 9)

Generous God,
    help us to sow bountifully
        as you have sown in us.
Let this time of worship nourish and inspire us,
    that we might share your many gifts
        with a world in need.
Let us be a giving people,
    sharing the love we have found in you
        with others.
Enrich us with your mercy.
Shower us with your grace,
    that we might shower this world
        with the abundance you have given to us.
In your gracious name, we pray. Amen.

PRAYER OF CONFESSION (2 CORINTHIANS 9)

Merciful God,
    we have not always been cheerful givers.
As we celebrate this day of thanksgiving,
    help us to turn our hearts back to you.
Forgive us for the many ways
    we hold on to your abundant gifts.
Loosen the chains that keep us from sharing with others
    as generously as you have shared with us.

Guide us that we might grow into the cheerful givers
and the grateful disciples you call us to be. Amen.

ASSURANCE OF PARDON (2 CORINTHIANS 9)

Hear this promise:
You will be enriched in every way
    for your great generosity.
God will supply your every need.
And because of the surpassing grace of God,
    we are forgiven for all of our sins.
In the name of Christ Jesus, we are forgiven!

BENEDICTION (LUKE 17)

Get up and go on your way.
Your faith has made you well!

BENEDICTION (DEUTERONOMY 8, PSALM 65, 2 CORINTHIANS 9)

Remember the Lord our God,
who has given us all we have.
**We go with the grace of Christ
to share all that God has bestowed on us.**
Take care to not forget,
God has given these gifts.
**We go with cheerful hearts
to share God's awesome love.**
Go and praise God's name!
**We go with singing hearts
to share God's gracious love!**

NOVEMBER 27, 2005

First Sunday of Advent
Crystal Sygeel

COLOR
Purple or Blue

SCRIPTURE READINGS
Isaiah 64:1-9; Psalm 80:1-7, 17-19; 1 Corinthians 1:3-9;
Mark 13:24-37

THEME IDEAS
Advent marks the time in the church when we wait and
prepare for God's arrival. The year has been long, and we
are weary, in need of rejuvenation, in need of salvation.
Advent is the darkest hour before the dawn. Winter
begins, nature withers and dies. But out of this cold
comes a warmth to revive our frozen hearts. Out of this
bleakness comes a beacon by which to steer our course in
faith. Out of chaos comes a sign of God's coming, a sign
of God's peace on earth.

CALL TO WORSHIP (ISAIAH 64)
Something is wrong;
  something has gone awry.
We are unclean,
  crooked and misshapen.
Our hearts are in knots,
  our thoughts a tangled mass.

God is hidden from us,
 like a figure enveloped in fog.
Like sun shrouded in cloud,
 we make our way to the Potter's wheel,
lie down on the circular plate,
 and wait for the artist's gentle hands.
As the wheel turns, the delicate push and pull
 smoothes out the cracks in our lives.
The wheel spins;
 Our souls are soothed.
We are reformed into new creatures—
 hands reaching, eyes raising—
To look in the eyes of God.
 Loving Potter, we are the clay; you are the artist.
 Come this morning and sculpt our hearts,
 mend our frayed lives, heal our wounds,
 and sand our rough edges.
 In this hour, restore our strength
 and make us whole.

CALL TO WORSHIP (ISAIAH 64)
Arise!
 Awake!
See, the season has turned.
 The time has now come.
The signs are everywhere,
 signaling God's arrival.
Like clay smoothed by the Potter,
 we will be reshaped, reborn.
We will dream; we will conceive
 of ideas great and small,
revisions, beginnings, a child.
 Loving God, entering Spirit,
 prepare us for the journey of Advent.
 Wake us from our spiritual slumber.
 Quicken us for the adventure
 of finding you born anew in our lives!

CALL TO WORSHIP

Keep awake!
You know not when God comes.
There will be signs:
A flood to cover the earth,
the red sea parting,
the walls of Jericho tumbling,
a giant slain by a boy,
a barren womb birthing a son,
a man sleeping in a den of lions,
another surviving the belly of a fish,
a virgin conceiving in her womb!
Keep awake!
God is coming!
Behold the signs!

CONTEMPORARY GATHERING WORDS (MARK 13)

And in these days there are signs that
God is coming:
Skies once filled with ash
have turned baby blue.
Cities bombed to rubble
are rebuilt and restored.
Families angry and silent
now reconnect and reconcile.
Nature once torn down and burned
is bringing forth new shoots.
Children lost and forgotten
are found and brought home.
Bones and bodies once sick with disease
find their parts surging with new life.
Lovers who quarreled away their love
reach out with new hope.
Countries once proud and unbending
are now peaceful and mending.

A star once shining in the midnight sky
  takes up her brilliance,
  shining once more.
God is coming!
Come and see the signs!

PRAISE SENTENCES (PSALM 80)

God comes to save us!
  Praise God whose face shines upon us!
God hears our every concern!
  Praise God who cares for us as a shepherd!
God comes to us in signs!
  Praise God whose light is coming into the world!

PRAISE SENTENCES (ISAIAH 64)

God is coming into the world!
  **Praise God who is doing miraculous
  and wondrous things!**
God is coming into the world!
  Praise God who shapes us as clay on the wheel.
God is coming into the world!
  Praise God who delivers us from danger!
God is coming into the world!
  **Praise God who tears open the sky
  and comes to us once more!**

OPENING PRAYER

God of eternity, God of now,
  make your signs visible to us.
Come into our world as you once did long ago.
Our world is in darkness,
  tear open the sky,
  flood the earth with your light!
Show us the life everlasting.
Show us the life now! Amen.

OPENING PRAYER

God of the journey, God of Advent,
    we come this morning looking for signs,
        signs of love, light, mercy, and forgiveness.
Come to us in this hour.
Be the candle that burns for us in the darkness.
Come into the night of our lives
    and be the sunlight that blooms for us! Amen.

PRAYER OF CONFESSION

We come this morning
    as a broken people, O God.
We have turned our lives from your path.
We do wrong against each other.
We choose apathy instead of activism.
We leave when we should stay.
We talk when we should listen.
We stiffen when we should bend.
We choose ourselves when we should choose you.
No wonder we are waiting for you to come.
No wonder we cannot take what is wrong
    and make it right.
We confess our sin,
    and we confess our need for your grace,
    your courage, and your tenderness.
Heal our wounds.
Bind our hearts.
And make us your people once more. Amen.

BENEDICTION

The blessings of God await those who watch
    and wait for the signs of Christ's coming.
Go forward into this day watching for the signs.
Go forward into this day and become signs
    for the whole world that Christ is coming.

DECEMBER 4, 2005

Second Sunday of Advent

Mary J. Scifres

COLOR

Purple or Blue

SCRIPTURE READINGS

Isaiah 40:1-11; Psalm 85:1-2, 8-13; 2 Peter 3:8-15*a*; Mark 1:1-8

THEME IDEAS

Preparing for Christ's coming is central in today's Advent readings. We prepare as a people of repentance (Mark). We prepare as a people of patience and godliness (1 Peter). We prepare as a people seeking justice and righteousness (Psalm 85). And, we prepare as a people who are comforted by Advent's promise of hope (Isaiah). These many ways of preparing—through repentance, patience, godliness, justice-seeking, righteousness, comfort, or hope—may be intertwined into a gentle theme of preparation. Or, any one of these themes may become the focus of today's worship.

CALL TO WORSHIP (ISAIAH 40, MARK 1)

Prepare the way of the Lord!
Make straight the pathway for our God.
Prepare the way of the Lord!

CALL TO WORSHIP (ISAIAH 40)

God speaks tenderly to us,
calling us into Christ's presence.
> **But not all of us are prepared**
> **to listen and respond.**

Prepare your ways, dear friends,
and make straight the paths of your lives.
> **Even as our lives twist and turn**
> **and pull us away from the Holy One?**

Even valleys can be lifted and mountains made low.
> **The uneven ground of our world can be leveled,**
and the rough roads of life can be smoothed.
> **We are here, seeking the comfort of God.**

God's comfort and glory have been revealed
in the Christmas promise.
> **And the Word of God has come into being.**
We are the people of God's promise.
> **We come to worship the God of promise.**

CALL TO WORSHIP (PSALM 85)

Look! Faithfulness and love meet in this place.
> **Righteousness and peace are present in our midst.**
The glory of God shines all around us.
> **The love of Jesus Christ flows through our lives.**
Listen! God is speaking peace to us all.
> **Come, let us worship God together.**

CALL TO WORSHIP (ADVENT)

December has come, and the winter winds blow.
> **Christ's birth and life seem so long ago.**
The birth of God's Son is celebrated anew.
> **Our faith and our hope are restored and renewed.**
God calls us to worship, to sing, and to pray.
> **We wait for the Holy One, on this the Lord's day.**

CONTEMPORARY GATHERING WORDS (ISAIAH 40, MARK 1)

Prepare the way of the Lord!
>**Prepare for Christ's place in our lives!**

Prepare the way of the Lord!
>**Prepare for Christ's place in our lives!**

CONTEMPORARY GATHERING WORDS (ISAIAH 40, 2 PETER 3)

We are waiting for Christ to come.
>**We are waiting with hope and joy!**

Christ's birthday is drawing near.
>**We are waiting with hope and joy!**

Prepare for the coming of God.
>**We are waiting with hope and joy!**

Worship and praise we bring.
>**We are waiting with hope and joy!**

PRAISE SENTENCES (PSALM 85)

Salvation is at hand. Glory to God!
>**Glory to God!**

PRAISE SENTENCES (PSALM 85, ADVENT)

Christ's hope is all around. Praise to the Holy One!
>**Praise to the Holy One!**

OPENING PRAYER (ISAIAH 40)

Gracious and mighty God,
>come to us with comfort and love.

Gather us into this place,
>that we might be one in your Holy Spirit.

Guide us in this time of worship,
>that we might hear and know your ways.

Lead us into new life,
that we might live as a people of hope.
In Christ's name, we pray. Amen.

OPENING PRAYER (2 PETER 3)
Come quickly, Lord Jesus.
Enter our world of strife and discord.
Infuse our lives with your spirit of peace and justice.
Engulf our worship with your loving presence
through the power of your Holy Spirit. Amen.

OPENING PRAYER (ADVENT)
God of past and present,
help us to prepare for the future.
As we remember your promises of days past,
help us to live your unchanging call
to love and forgive.
As we reflect on the prophecies of Advent,
help us to prepare for the coming of Christ.
As we worship your holy presence,
help us to worship in spirit and truth. Amen.

CALL TO CONFESSION (MARK 1)
As we prepare to receive Christ into our lives,
let us pray for the forgiveness of our sins.

PRAYER OF CONFESSION (2 PETER 3, ADVENT)
Holy and righteous God,
you call us to be blameless and good.
We desire to be at peace,
but are haunted by our impatience
and our many imperfections.
Help us to be patient with ourselves and others.
Guide us into total trust of your perfect love.
Straighten the paths of our lives,
that we may see your way,

directly and clearly.
Calm our worried souls,
    that we may find patience and peace.
Grant us faith and courage,
    that we may know unfailing trust and hope.
Love us in this season,
    that we may celebrate Christmas
        with joy and thanksgiving.
In the name of Christ,
    your child on this earth,
    we pray. Amen.

WORDS OF ASSURANCE (ISAIAH 40)
Comfort, O comfort, you people of God.
Christ comes with mighty love.
The Good Shepherd gathers us gently in.
With shepherding love, we are nurtured and fed.
With overwhelming grace,
    we are forgiven again and again.

BENEDICTION (ISAIAH 40)
Grass may wither, but God's Word endures forever.
**Flowers may fade, but the promises of Christ
live faithfully through the years.**
Go forth, proclaiming the good news of God's love.
**We lift our voices with strength.
We lift God's love with joy!**

BENEDICTION (2 PETER 3)
Christ is coming soon.
Christ's love is here even now.
Take God's love into the world.
We carry God's love as we leave.

DECEMBER 11, 2005

Third Sunday of Advent
B. J. Beu

COLOR

Purple or Blue

SCRIPTURE READINGS

Isaiah 61:1-4, 8-11; Psalm 126; 1 Thessalonians 5:16-24; John 1:6-8, 19-28

THEME IDEAS

Walk in darkness no longer, for the God of redeeming love has brought the fullness of God's light into the world. The same Spirit to which Isaiah testified and to which the psalmist celebrated has brought us joy in the coming of Christ. John the Baptist testified to the light of God, and we receive this light when we welcome Christ into our hearts and proclaim release to the captives, good news to the oppressed, and the year of the Lord's favor.

CALL TO WORSHIP (ISAIAH 61)

God has anointed us to bring good news
to all people.
 The Spirit of the Lord is upon us!
Let us proclaim good news to the oppressed
and liberty to the captives.
 The Spirit of the Lord is upon us!
Let us bind up the wounds of the afflicted
and comfort those who mourn.

The Spirit of the Lord is upon us!
Let us proclaim the year of the Lord's favor
and release to the prisoners.
The Spirit of the Lord is upon us!
Let us be known as oaks of righteousness,
the plantings of the Lord.
The Spirit of the Lord is upon us!

CALL TO WORSHIP (PSALM 126)

We are like those who dream.
God has restored our fortunes!
Laugh for all the world to hear.
Let the nations hear our shouts of joy!
The Lord has done great things for us.
Our tears of sorrow have become tears of joy!
Let us worship the Lord our God.

CONTEMPORARY GATHERING WORDS (1 THESSALONIANS 5)

God's love has called us here.
Rejoice in the Lord always.
Pray with unceasing hope.
Let the world know the greatness of our God.
Rejoice in the Lord always.
Pray with unceasing hope.
Christ has called us here,
promising perfect love and grace.
Rejoice in the Lord always.
Pray with unceasing hope.
Come before God with open hearts
and joyful words.
Rejoice in the Lord always.
Pray with unceasing hope.

PRAISE SENTENCES (ISAIAH 61, JOHN 1)

Rejoice in the Lord!
Revel in God's glory.

God has clothed us in salvation!
The darkness of night is over.
Salvation is at hand!
Rejoice as children of light!

PRAISE SENTENCES (PSALM 126)

O God, your love surrounds us.
Your faithfulness restores our life.
You fill our hearts with laughter.
You fill our mouths with shouts of joy.
O God, we sing your praises.

OPENING PRAYER (ISAIAH 61)

Spirit of God,
    you clothe us with the garments of salvation,
        as a bride is adorned with jewels.
Make us instruments of your mercy,
    that we might lead others to experience your kingdom
        here on earth.
Anoint us to be messengers of your good news—
    the brokenhearted will be comforted;
    the captives will be set free;
    the sick will be healed;
    and the needy will find abundance
        in the year of the Lord's favor. Amen.

OPENING PRAYER (JOHN 1)

Eternal God,
    you bring light out of darkness
    and hope out of despair.
Share your love with us this day
    that we may better love each other.
Touch our hearts with the joy of Advent,
    and help our love shine forth
        in a world hungry to know your love.
In Jesus' name we pray. Amen.

PRAYER OF CONFESSION (JOHN 1)
Christ of light and life,
John the Baptist came before you,
to prepare our hearts
for your arrival in our world.
For the times when we act as if your light has not come,
forgive us.
For the days when we choose darkness over your light,
forgive us.
For the ways in which we shun your prophets,
forgive us.
Guide us, we pray, to see your glory,
full of grace and truth. Amen.

WORDS OF ASSURANCE (JOHN 1)
Children of God,
Christ has made straight the paths to God.
The light of the world has come
to lead us from our darkness
into the light of God's love.
Receive the fullness of Christ's grace
and know that you are forgiven.

BENEDICTION (1 THESSALONIANS 5)
May the unquenchable Spirit of God sanctify you entirely,
and may your soul and body be kept blameless
at the coming of our Lord Jesus Christ. Amen.

BENEDICTION (JOHN 1)
Walk in darkness no longer.
We will walk in the light of Christ.
Make straight the way of the Lord.
We will prepare the way of the Lord.
Receive the good news of God's love.
**We will receive God's blessings
and share it with the world.**

DECEMBER 18, 2005

Fourth Sunday of Advent
Judy Schultz

COLOR
Purple or Blue

SCRIPTURE READINGS
2 Samuel 7:1-11, 16; Luke 1:47-55; Romans 16:25-27; Luke 1:26-38

THEME IDEAS
Nothing is impossible with God, not even God's birth as a human being. Themes for this day can be those of awe and wonder at the angelic message; the faithful agreement of Mary, who exhibits the "obedience of faith" to which Paul refers; or the new, never-ending kingdom that will be inaugurated, where those who are humble will be lifted up, the hungry fed, and God's promises fulfilled.

CALL TO WORSHIP (ROMANS 16, LUKE 1)
Greetings, people of God!
You have found favor with God!
We wonder what sort of greeting this is,
for we are ordinary people.
You are special people!
God has chosen you to see the revelation of a mystery,
the coming birth of the Messiah.
God's wisdom and works are astonishing.

To God be glory forever!
Let us worship God.

CALL TO WORSHIP (2 SAMUEL 7)

Come and worship.
Hear the voice of an angel announcing good news.
We come to worship this day with great expectation.
Come and worship.
Our dwelling is about to become the house of God.
We come to worship singing praises to God.
Come and worship.
A great secret is about to be told.
**We come to worship the God whom Christ reveals.
Praise God!**

PRAISE SENTENCES (LUKE 1)

The humble are exalted; the proud are humiliated.
Praise God!
The hungry are fed; the gluttons are turned away.
Praise God!
The lowly are raised up; the arrogant are ignored.
Praise God for the new kingdom coming to birth!

PRAISE SENTENCES (ROMANS 16)

We have a secret to tell. We have a mystery to reveal.
It's good news for everyone. God is within us.
God is in Jesus. God is coming again to dwell with us,
to dwell within us. Expect a miracle! Expect God!

OPENING PRAYER (LUKE 1)

Holy and amazing God,
whom an angel announced,
you come first to the lowly and the meek.
Surprise us, we pray,
with your gracious Spirit
in our worship this day,
and in our lives forever. Amen.

OPENING PRAYER (LUKE 1)

Holy God, hidden yet revealed,
  come again to your people and dwell among us.
Open our hearts to receive you.
Prepare our lives to enact in word and deed
  your amazing, upside-down kingdom,
    where the humble are exalted,
    the poor are made rich,
    and all who hunger for your Spirit
    are satisfied. Amen.

BENEDICTION (ROMANS 16, LUKE 1)

Go now from this place of worship
  in the strength of God's love
  and in the promise that Christ is coming anew.
Live expectantly and faithfully.
And listen for the voice of an angel.

BENEDICTION (LUKE 1)

As you leave this place,
  may the words of the angel ring in your ears.
You have found favor with God.
God is coming to you.
God wants to bring new life to birth within you.
Live expectantly. Live confidently.
Live in God's favor and God's love.

BENEDICTION (ROMANS 16, LUKE 1)

As you go from this place,
know you have found favor with God.
  We are amazed at this great honor,
  but we will strive to believe it.
Your belief must be turned into words and actions.
  We will seek to live in obedience to our beliefs.
God will strengthen you in will and spirit.
  We know that nothing is impossible with God.

DECEMBER 24, 2005

Christmas Eve
Mary J. Scifres

COLOR
White

SCRIPTURE READINGS
Isaiah 9:2-7; Psalm 96; Titus 2:11-14; Luke 2:1-14 (15-20)

THEME IDEAS
Christmas Eve is a time of grace and love, light and hope. The promises of Christmas are reflected in scripture in rich and unique ways: Isaiah's promise of light after darkness; the psalmist's joy in God whose salvation is mighty and strong; Titus's proclamation of grace; and Luke's beloved rendition of that first Christmas, filled with angels of hope and signs of God's love. This service is a time to reflect on the promises of Christmas in word and music, in ritual and celebration. Christ is born! Glory to God in the highest!

CALL TO WORSHIP (ISAIAH 9, LUKE 2)
We once walked in darkness,
but tonight we walk in light.
We once lived in sorrow,
but tonight we live in joy!
Our burdens have been lifted
and laid in a manger of love.

December 24, 2005

A child has given us hope, mercy,
grace, and peace.
We gather this evening
with thanks and praise,
to witness the gift of a baby,
Christ Jesus, the promised one,
the light of God's redeeming love.
We rejoice in God's miraculous gift!

CALL TO WORSHIP (PSALM 96, LUKE 2)

Sing a new song to God!
Bless God's holy name!
Glorify the greatness of God,
the love we've waited for.
Strength and beauty are born this night,
incarnate in a tiny child.
Christ is truly king,
the judge of all the earth.
Sing a new song to God!
For on Christmas, God sang to us!

CONTEMPORARY GATHERING WORDS (LUKE 2)

We bring good news this day,
Jesus Christ is born!
Jesus Christ is born!
Glory to God in the highest!
Christ brings peace and hope,
the love of God on earth!
Jesus Christ is born!
Glory to God in the highest!

PRAISE SENTENCES (PSALM 96)

Sing to the Lord a new song!
We sing a new song to God!
Sing to the Lord a new song!
We sing a new song to God!

259

PRAISE SENTENCES (TITUS 2)

Love has come, grace is all around!
Love has come, grace is all around!
Jesus Christ is love, God's grace given to us!
Jesus Christ is love, God's grace given to us!

OPENING PRAYER (TITUS 2, LUKE 2)

Holy Child,
  we come to your manger on this Christmas Eve,
  filled with wonder and awe
    for your presence among us.
As you came to us on that first Christmas Eve,
  come to us now.
Enter our hearts and our worship,
  that we might recognize the shining light
    of your love and grace.
In your loving name we pray. Amen.

OPENING PRAYER (ISAIAH 9)

God of light and love,
  shine upon us this Christmas Eve
    and in the year ahead.
Guide us out of darkness
  and into your joyous light.
May our lives reflect your glorious love,
  that others may see your Christmas Spirit in us,
    tonight and all nights. Amen.

BENEDICTION (ISAIAH 9, TITUS 2)

Walk in light with Christ.
  Shine with glorious hope.
Love with the grace of God.
  Live with the love of Christ.

BENEDICTION (PSALM 96)

Christ is born!
Go forth with Christ's song in your heart!
  Christ is born!
  We'll live with God's love in our lives!

DECEMBER 25, 2005

Christmas Day
Mary J. Scifres

COLOR
White

SCRIPTURE READINGS
Isaiah 52:7-10; Psalm 98; Hebrews 1:1-4 (5-12); John 1:1-14

THEME IDEAS
The birth of Jesus is only the beginning of today's themes. Grace and salvation flow outward from this miracle of the Christian faith and permeate the scripture readings. Our need to sing and rejoice in response to that gift is expressed in word and song throughout the Christmas season. These scriptures remind us that those needs are as ancient as the Word of God itself. Let scripture's poetry fill today's worship services; allow the words and images to fill the room and the souls of everyone present.

CALL TO WORSHIP (JOHN 1)
In the beginning was the Word.
   And the Word was with God.
And the Word was God.
   Christ is our Word, given from the beginning.
The light of God has shone in the darkness.
   Christ is our light, shining with all glory.
Christ has come, full of grace and truth.
   Praise be! Christ is with us even now!

CALL TO WORSHIP (PSALM 98)

Sing to the Lord a new song!
For God has done marvelous things!
God has revealed the victory of love through Christ
Jesus.
**God has remembered us with faithful love,
a love that never ends.**
Make a joyful noise to God, all the earth!
We sing with praise and joy on this Christmas day!

CONTEMPORARY GATHERING WORDS

Love has come!
Christ is born!
Love is all around!
Christ is born!
Love is ours!
Christ is born!

CONTEMPORARY GATHERING WORDS (JOHN 1)

The light of God is shining.
Christ is our light!
The light shines in even the darkest places.
Christ is our light!
The true light lives among us.
Christ is our light!
The light of God is full of grace and truth.
Christ is our light!
Thanks be to God.

PRAISE SENTENCES (PSALM 98)

Sing to the Lord a new song!
We sing a new song to God!
Sing to the Lord a new song!
We sing a new song to God!

OPENING PRAYER (ISAIAH 52)

How beautiful is your messenger
sent this Christmas day!
For bringing good news and the promise of peace,
   we thank you, Redeemer God.
As we worship the Christ Child this day,
   may our voices burst forth
      into song full of joy and hope.
Turn the words of our mouths
   into actions of peace and comfort
      for a world in need of your joy and hope.
May our deeds open doors of salvation and grace
   to those around us,
   that your good news and promised peace
      might become the way of this world.
In Christ's precious name, we pray. Amen.

OPENING PRAYER (JOHN 1)

Light of God,
   as you came on that Christmas morning
      so many years ago, come to us this day.
Gather us into your light and love.
Fill us with your brightness and glory.
Shine over us with your love and grace.
Help us to know you and to love you
   in all that we say and all that we do. Amen.

PRAYER OF CONFESSION AND ASSURANCE (HEBREWS 1)

Loving God,
   we thank you for sending us your very self
   in the person of Jesus.
When we neglect or deny your gift,
   forgive us.
Purify our hearts, purge our sins,
   and make us your children.

Help us to see Christ
    as the reflection of your glory and majesty.
Help us to love righteousness,
    even as we reject all injustice and oppression.
Through your child Jesus,
    may we come to know you more fully,
    that we may live as your children,
        full of righteousness and grace, love and joy.
In the name of Jesus the Son, we pray. Amen.

WORDS OF ASSURANCE (PSALM 98, HEBREWS 1)

Christ has come to judge with righteousness and equity.
Christ has come to love with grace and mercy.
Through the gracious gift of God,
    and the gift of Christ Jesus, we are forgiven!

BENEDICTION (ISAIAH 52)

How blessed is the messenger who announces peace.
Go, therefore, and be messengers of peace!
    We go to proclaim the good news of Christ's birth!
Sing of salvation and peace.
    We will live with grace and joy.
In our lives, may others see God in plain sight.
    In our love, may others know Christ's compassion.
Go, my friends, and be messengers of that peace,
which passes all understanding, the peace that is ours
through Christ Jesus, our redeemer and our joy.

BENEDICTION (PSALM 98)

Sing to God with joy and praise!
    Even as we depart, we can sing of Christ's birth.
The mountains and hills are alive with joy on this day.
    May our lives speak as joyously and faithfully
    as the works of God's creation.
Go with joy, for Christ is with us!
    Amen.

CONTRIBUTORS

LAURA JAQUITH BARTLETT serves as minister of music in the Oregon-Idaho Conference of The United Methodist Church, where she also spends time as a leader in outdoor ministry, raising two daughters, and learning to play the djembe.

ROBERT BLEZARD is a writer and editor for the Evangelical Lutheran Church of America, with his home base in Gettysburg, Pennsylvania.

CHRISTINE S. BOARDMAN is a professional singer in her earlier life but now specializes in interim judicatory ministry in the United Church of Christ.

KEVIN C. BOGAN is the Director of Music at Central United Methodist Church in Fayetteville, Arkansas, and a Council member of the Fellowship of United Methodists in Music and Worship Arts.

MARY PETRINA BOYD is a pastor serving Coupeville United Methodist Church on Whidbey Island in Puget Sound. She spends alternate summers digging at Tal al 'Umayri, an archaeological site in Jordan.

JOHN A. BREWER pastors Salmon Creek United Methodist Church in Vancouver, Washington, after serving eight years as district superintendent.

JOANNE CARLSON BROWN is a United Methodist minister serving at United Church in University Place, Washington, and an adjunct faculty member of church history and historical theology at the School of Theology and Ministry, Seattle University.

REBECCA GAUDINO is a United Church of Christ pastor in Portland, Oregon.

NANCY CRAWFORD HOLM received her Master of Arts degree in Pastoral Studies from Seattle University and is chairman of the Board of Directors of the Grünewald Guild, a community dedicated to nurturing the connections between art and faith.

HANS HOLZNAGEL lives on the Near West Side of Cleveland, Ohio, where he is a member of Archwood United Church of Christ. He has served as a journalist, administrator, and public relations officer with mission agencies of the United Church of Christ for twenty years.

BILL HOPPE is the music coordinator and keyboardist for Bear Creek United Methodist Church in Woodinville, Washington, and is also a friend of Aslan.

KRISTI HANSON KREAMER serves as pastor at Christ Lutheran Church, Lakewood, Washington.

SARA DUNNING LAMBERT loves God and her family and enjoys sharing music, shepherding youth, exploring creativity, and playing with friends.

PAULA MCCUTCHEON is currently copastoring Fairwood Community United Methodist Church with her spouse, James Clarke.

RANDY L. ROWLAND is an ordained minister in the Presbyterian Church (USA). He is author of several books, a columnist for *Worship Leader Magazine* and currently Academic Dean of Northwest Graduate School in Seattle, Washington.

JUDY SCHULTZ, a self-professed late-bloomer, is pastor of Haller Lake United Methodist Church in Seattle, Washington.

LEONARD SWEET serves as the E. Stanley Jones Professor of Evangelism at Drew Theological School, while continuing his work as a writer and preacher. His homiletic work can be found at preachingplus.com.

CRYSTAL SYGEEL has been a liturgical artist for eighteen years and is currently serving as diaconal minister for First United Methodist Church in Bellevue, Washington.

LAWRENCE WIK is a United Methodist pastor and an active musician. With his wife, Jennifer, he parents three young children.

BRIAN WREN is a hymnwriter, minister, and professor of worship at Columbia Theological Seminary, Decatur, Georgia.

SCRIPTURE INDEX